Popular Mechanics

Car Owner's Companion

101 Things You Need to Know

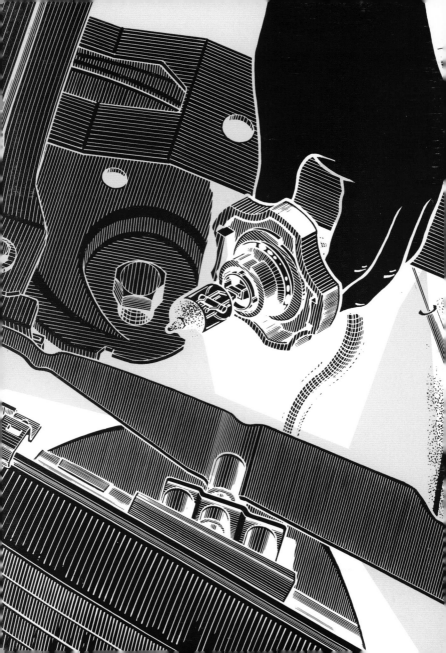

Popular Mechanics

Car Owner's Companion

101 Things You Need to Know

Bob Freudenberger

WITHDRAWN

Hearst Books

A Division of Sterling Publishing Co., Inc.

New York

Library of Congress Cataloging-in-Publication Data
Freudenberger, Bob.
Popular mechanics car owner's
companion: 101 things you need to know /
Bob Freudenberger.
    p. cm.
 Includes bibliographical references and
index.
  ISBN 1-58816-213-3 (alk. paper)
 1. Automobiles—Maintenance and
repair—Popular works. 2. Automobile
ownership—Popular works. I. Title: Car
owner's companion. II. Popular
mechanics (Chicago, Ill.: 1959) III. Title.
  TL152.F7286 2006

                629.28'72—dc22
                2005013111

10 9 8 7 6 5 4 3 2 1

Photos by Bob Freudenberger.

Illustrations by Russell J. Von Sauers,
Ron Carbone, and Don Mannes.

Published by Hearst Books
A Division of Sterling Publishing Co., Inc.
387 Park Avenue South
New York, NY 10016

Popular Mechanics and
Hearst Books are trademarks of
Hearst Communications, Inc.

www.popularmechanics.com

For information about custom editions,
special sales, premium and corporate
purchases, please contact Sterling Special
Sales Department at 800-805-5489 or
specialsales@sterlingpub.com.

Distributed in Canada by Sterling
Publishing
^{c}/o Canadian Manda Group,
165 Dufferin Street
Toronto, Ontario, Canada M6K 3H6

Distributed in Australia by Capricorn Link
(Australia) Pty. Ltd.
P.O. Box 704, Windsor, NSW 2756
Australia

Manufactured in China

Sterling ISBN 13: 978-158816-213-7
     ISBN 10: 1-58816-213-3

Table of Contents

Foreword 9

Introduction 10

Section 1
Orientation 11

Getting Comfortable 12
  1. Opening the hood 12
  2. Mechanical tour 14
  3. Fluids: Keeping the
    levels up 24
  4. Battery terminals 27
  5. Accessory drive belts 29
  6. Radiator hoses 30
  7. Radiator 31
  8. Air filter and ducts 31

Section 2
Breakdowns 33

*Management and Safety
Strategies* 34
  9. The car is your safe
    haven 34
  10. If you *must* get
out . . . 34
  11. Who to call 35

Won't Go 36
  12. No-crank or no-fire
    starting failures 36
  13. Jump-starting 39
  14. Charging a battery 40
  15. Installing a new battery 41
  16. Sudden stop 43
  17. No power to the wheels 43

Flat Tire 45
  18. Spares 45
  19. Don't get squashed! Safe
    changing procedures 46
  20. Inflators 50
  21. Practice ahead of time 50

Leaks 51
  22. Coolant (antifreeze) 51
  23. Motor oil 52
  24. Automatic transmission
    fluid (ATF) 54
  25. Power steering fluid 55
  26. Brake fluid 56

SOS: Warning Lamps 57
  27. Charging system 57
  28. Oil pressure 58
  29. Check engine 59
  30. Brake or ABS lamp 61

Section 3
No Fun to Drive?   63

Not-So-Petty Annoyances   64
  31. Wander   64
  32. Pulling to one side   67
  33. Bad vibes   69
  34. Bouncing and leaning   70
  35. Brake pulsation   71
  36. Rough idle   73
  37. Sluggish performance   74
Noises   76
  38. Pad wear indicator   76
  39. Clunks and thumps   77
  40. Tapping/knocking   80
  41. Rattles and buzzes   81
Bad Smells   85
  42. Cleanliness, water leaks, and mildew   85
  43. From the A/C?   87
  44. Smoke and filters   89

Section 4
Driving Tips   91

Take It Easy   92
  45. Defensive driving   92
Slippery Conditions   93
  46. Skid physics   93
  47. Installing tire chains   94
Saving Money   95
  48. Calculating fuel mileage   95
  49. Easy acceleration   96

  50. Reduced cruising speed   96
Accidents   97
  51. Don't move   97
  52. Fire   97
  53. Mayday!   98
  54. Mum's the word   99
  55. In the drink   99
Keys, Doors, Hatches, and Windows   101
  56. Can't turn the ignition key?   101
  57. Hiding a spare key   102
  58. Key fobs and remotes   103
  59. Door-latch strikers   104
  60. Sagging hatch and hood supports   105
  61. Power windows   106
  62. Power locks   108
See and Be Seen   109
  63. Wipers   109
  64. Windshield washers   111
  65. That tenacious windshield haze   112
  66. Windshield bull's-eyes   113
  67. Reattaching the rearview mirror   114
Headlights   116
  68. Sealed beam   116
  69. Composite   117

70. High-intensity discharge 118
71. Signal lights 119

Section 5
Maintenance Matters 121

They Last and Last 122

72. The truth about durability 122

Engine and Transmission 124

73. Oil changes 124
74. Coolant changes 127
75. Today's tune-up 129
76. The truth about spark plugs 130
77. Timing-belt replacement 131
78. Transmission fluid changes 131

Tires 133

79. Inflation 133
80. Rotation 133
81. Buying tires 134
82. Brake fluid changes 136

Body 138

83. Washing and waxing 138
84. Paint chips 141
85. Rust spots 142
86. Drain holes 144
87. Dealing with professionals 144

Section 6
Miscellaneous 149

Random, but Important 150

88. What to carry with you 150
89. Battery parasitic drain 152
90. Gasoline goes stale 153
91. Interior mildew 154
92. Buying gasoline 155
93. When the battery must be disconnected . . . 156
94. Warranties 157
95. Fail an emissions test? 161

Exhaust System 166

96. Rattles 166
97. Leaks 167
98. Temporary fix 168

Where to Get Info 168

99. If you've lost your owner's manual 168
100. Factory service manuals 169
101. Aftermarket tech info 170

Car Care Log 172
Dedication 173
Index 174

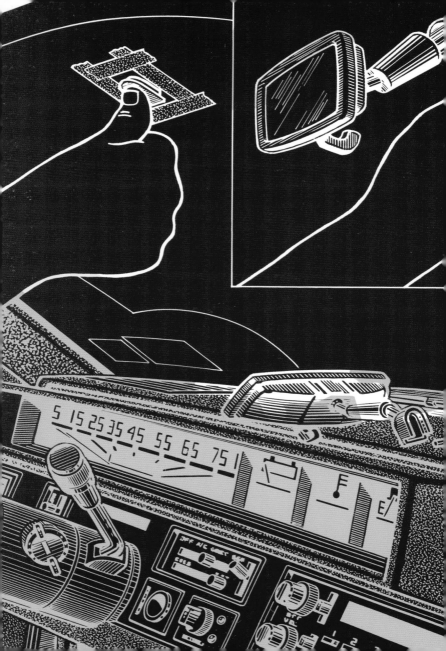

Foreword

For over a century, *Popular Mechanics* has helped its readers understand the technology of the world around them. And throughout that period there has been no technology more vital to daily life than the car and truck. Of course, motor vehicles have become infinitely more complex since those early days. Today's vehicles incorporate a range of digital technology, exotic materials, and engineering breakthroughs that would have been inconceivable even a few decades ago.

As a result of those refinements, many people believe that maintaining and repairing the typical late-model car is well beyond the abilities of the do-it-yourselfer. We at *Popular Mechanics* take a very different view. Yes, it's true there are many sealed components under the hood today. And some of the familiar, easy-to-tinker-with items found on classic cars are long gone. But there's still plenty that a car owner can do to keep the family car or truck in prime condition. All you need is the knowledge and the desire. With this book, based on our years of expert advice on auto service, we're providing the knowledge. It's up to you to provide the desire.

Jim Meigs
Editor-in-Chief

Introduction

In spite of our society's abject dependence on motor vehicles, the average person doesn't really know that much about owning, operating, and maintaining his or her car, and has no plan of action for breakdowns and emergencies. Your owner's manual is a good source of information—as far as it goes. But, there are none with magazine readability, or logical organization that fits the vagaries of the real world.

Hence, this book. Hopefully, you'll actually enjoy reading it so that maybe you'll do so *before* a crisis occurs. It has been arranged so that you won't have to look in seemingly unrelated sections to find the information you might need at any given time. Take a minute to look over the table of contents and you'll see what we mean.

Follow the advice in this book and you'll save money and frustration, enjoy your motoring experiences more than ever before, handle emergencies with wisdom and aplomb, and, years from now, you'll be pleasantly surprised at how well your car is holding up.

Orientation

Getting Comfortable

1. Opening the hood

No, we're not making fun of your mechanical disinclination. It's a joke even in service shops that sometimes you just can't find that safety catch. On the other hand, the lever or handle inside of the car is obvious. It's typically to the left of the steering column at the lower edge of the dashboard, and it'll either say "Hood," or have a drawing of an automobile with its hood up. Pull it until you hear a bump, which means a coil spring has popped the hood up against the safety catch.

Now, put your fingers inside the gap between the hood and the grille and feel around. In most cases, you'll encounter a lever toward the center

>> **Hood release**

somewhere. Push the hood down a little to take the spring pressure off the catch, then move the lever sideways, in or out, or up or down (whichever works) and raise the hood. Some cars have the safety catch down in the middle of the grille, and others have a tab that sticks out, which you pull. Of course, you could look this up in your owner's manual and perhaps save yourself some frustration.

>> **Hood safety catch**

>> **Hood prop**

Some vehicles have a system of springs and levers or pneumatic cylinders that hold the hood up, while others depend on a simple prop or strut. In the latter case, unhook the prop from its hood-down position, raise it and insert it into the appropriate hole on the underside of the hood, which is usually indicated by an arrow or label.

EXTRA: Don't Bend the Hood

After doing anything in the engine compartment, make sure you look around before you close the hood. A tool or even a fluid container in the wrong place can result in a bent hood and the need for bodywork.

2. Mechanical tour

Looking around under the hood can be interesting if you take the time to try to understand how each component fits into the grand scheme of motorized transportation.

>> Engine oil dipstick

The **oil dipstick** fits in a tube that goes down into the engine crankcase. It's labeled "Oil," or has an oil can logo. Some late models have dispensed with this traditional item in favor of an electronic system that lets you know how much oil is in the crankcase. Look it up in your owner's manual if you're unsure.

Your car probably has an **automatic transmission**. If so, there'll be a dipstick for that, too, with a thicker tube than that for the oil, that fits into the transmission.

The **coolant overflow reservoir** holds extra antifreeze and water. It's usually made of translucent plastic and is connected to the radiator cap neck with a small hose. On many late models, this is pressurized, so the traditional radiator cap is here instead of on top of the radiator.

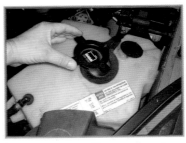

>> **Coolant overflow reservoir**

>> **Windshield washer fluid reservoir**

Don't confuse this reservoir with the **windshield washer fluid reservoir**, which may look similar. Examine the symbols on the caps carefully.

Brake fluid level is important for safety. Most modern cars have a brake **master cylinder** with a plastic reservoir. The round, steel chamber behind the master cylinder is the **power brake booster**, which operates on the vacuum the engine creates.

>> **Brake master cylinder**

Cars with **power steering** have a belt-driven pump to supply hydraulic pressure for this option. A screw cap, with the fluid-level dipstick attached, seals the reservoir. Which may or may not be on the pump.

>> **Power steering pump**

A pleated paper-like **air filter element** is used to keep dust, dirt, and insects out of the engine's intake stream. It's commonly found inside a big plastic box that's connected to the engine's throttle body (at or near the top of the engine, the assembly controls the amount of air ingested for combustion—the throttle is a rotating "door" attached to the gas pedal) by means of a large-diameter rubber or plastic duct. On older models, it's inside a metal housing that sits right on top of the **carburetor** or fuel injection **throttle body**.

Almost all cars old enough to have a **carburetor** use a **mechanical fuel pump** to bring gasoline from the tank. It's mounted on the side of the engine block and forces fuel through a small steel pipe and a filter up into the carburetor. Vehicles with **fuel injection** (most passenger vehicles on the road today), on the other hand, have an **electric fuel pump** mounted in or near the gas tank, and the filter may be there, along a chassis rail, or in the engine compartment.

>> Oil filter

The **oil filter** screws onto the side of the engine block and is replaced when the oil is changed. In some cases you can reach it from the top, in others you'll have to get underneath.

At the front of the engine (with front-wheel-drive/transverse-engine configurations, this will be toward the side of the car) you'll see the belt or belts that transmit power from the crankshaft pulley to the accessories, including the alternator, water and power steering pumps, air conditioning compressor, etc. Late models have a single, flat **serpentine belt** with multiple-V-grooves or ribs on the working side.

>> **Serpentine accessory drivebelt**

The **radiator** dissipates the engine's waste heat to the atmosphere. It's mounted at the front of the engine compartment and is connected to the cooling system with two big rubber hoses. Smaller hoses conduct the coolant to the **heater core** in the passenger compartment.

EXTRA: Scalding Geyser

>> **Radiator cap**

Never open the **radiator cap** when the engine's hot! Since the cooling system is pressurized, the water and antifreeze mixture inside can be kept at a temperature higher than the boiling point, which means a superheated geyser will spew out with great force if the cap is removed, scalding anybody nearby.

>> Valve cover

On top of the **cylinder head** or heads, there's what is variously called a **valve**, **rocker**, or **camshaft cover**. It may be made

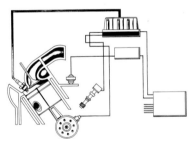

>> Distributorless ignition systems use an electronic coil module, and camshaft, crankshaft, and detonation sensors to provide spark. There's no distributor, distributor cap or rotor.

of sheet metal, cast aluminum or magnesium, or plastic, and the seam between it and the head is a common oil-leak point.

The cast iron or steel tubing part that's bolted to the side of the head and points downward is the **exhaust manifold**, which channels waste gases and heat through a pipe to the **catalytic converter** and the **muffler**. Watch it—it's hot.

The **spark plugs** screw into the cylinder head, and ignite the air/fuel mixture in the combustion chamber. They get high voltage from the **distributor** or **distributorless-ignition** unit through wires that are typically 7 or 8 mm in diameter and have rubber boots at their ends. Or, in many late models with direct ignition systems, there are small wires running to an **ignition coil** at the top of each plug.

The small-diameter rubber hoses you may see in various locations are **vacuum lines**. They route the vacuum that the engine creates as its pistons descend on the intake stroke to various emission-control devices and accessories. If these lines come loose or crack, a vacuum leak can affect how the engine runs. Sometimes there's a diagram under the hood that shows where they're connected.

>> With direct ignition, no high-voltage ignition wires are needed since there's a coil at each spark plug.

>> **PCV valve**

The **Positive Crankcase Ventilation** (PCV) valve is important because it allows corrosive, sludge-forming fumes to be drawn out of the crankcase into the cylinders to be burned. It's usually found plugged into a rubber grommet in the valve cover (also known as the rocker or camshaft cover). Some engines use a liquid/vapor separator for this function, so they don't have a PCV valve.

>> **Alternator**

The **alternator** is what provides electrical power for lights and accessories. It also keeps the battery charged. It's driven by a crankshaft pulley belt, which may be either a single serpentine belt or one of multiple V- or flat microV-belts.

The voltage it produces is kept at the proper level by a **voltage regulator**, which may be inside the alternator itself, mounted remotely, or incorporated into the engine management system computer.

Usually located toward the bottom of the engine compartment, the **starter** is a heavy electric motor that cranks the engine when you twist the key. It has a **solenoid** (a remotely controlled electrical switch) mounted on it or elsewhere, that switches the heavy current needed.

>> This battery has both top and side terminals.

The **battery** is actually a reservoir of electrical power. It's connected to the starter and electrical system by means of a heavy **positive cable**, and to the engine block or cylinder head with an equally heavy **negative cable**, which provides the ground path necessary for a complete circuit. The condition of the connection between the battery posts and the cable clamps is critical.

In most vehicles, the battery is located under the hood on either side of the engine, at the front or the back, but there are examples of the battery being mounted in the trunk or under the back seat (as in the old Volkswagen Type 1 Beetle).

Back on the **firewall** (the steel bulkhead that is between the engine compartment and the passenger cabin) is the **windshield wiper motor**, which runs on electricity, or, in very old cars, on the vacuum the engine produces.

>> **Fuses and relays**

Many late-model cars have a box under the hood that contains major **fuses** and **relays**, such as those for the fuel pump. Other fuses and relays are under the dash by the steering column.

At the lower end of the steering column, you'll find the mechanism that translates steering-wheel movement into front-wheel movement. Called, logically enough, the **steering gear**, it may be of the **rack-and-pinion** type, or of the **recirculating ball** variety, which you'll find mostly on large domestic cars and trucks.

If your car has a manual transmission, it naturally has a **clutch**. The pedal should have a certain amount of free play, which is easily adjustable on the cable- or linkage-actuated type. Hydraulically controlled clutches don't normally need adjustment.

3. Fluids: Keeping the levels up

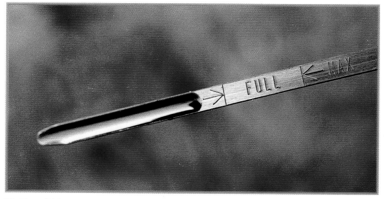

>> **Read the crankcase oil level on the dipstick.**

T o check the oil, park the car on a level surface and let it sit for a few minutes to allow the circulating oil to drain back into the crankcase. Then, remove the dipstick, wipe it off, reinsert it all the way, pull it out again, hold it parallel to the ground, and look at the level on the end of the stick. Markings on the dipstick will tell you if

the crankcase is full or not. If it's below the Full mark, it's time to add oil.

You'll find a cap, typically identified with an oil-can symbol, right on top of the engine in the valve or camshaft cover. It'll either unlock with a quarter turn counter-clockwise, or unscrew. Pour the oil into the hole. The cutoff top of a

>> **Remove this cap to pour in the motor oil.**

clean plastic soda bottle makes a good disposable funnel. Don't overfill as this will cause foaming and poor lubricant distribution.

With the engine cool, see if the level in the coolant reservoir is between the Full and Low or Hot and Cold marks. No? Then remove the radiator cap and top up the level with a mixture of one-half the recommended type of antifreeze and one-half distilled or deionized water. Bring the level in the coolant reservoir up to the middle, too. *Never open the radiator cap when*

the engine is hot or you could end up in a burn center.

In most cases, the fluid level in the transmission should be checked after driving so that everything is at normal operating temperature. Park the car on a level surface and keep it idling in Park. Use the automatic transmission dipstick to check the fluid level as you did for the oil.

Add Automatic Transmission Fluid (ATF) through the dipstick tube—you may need a funnel with an extension hose. Just as with the engine, be careful not to overfill.

With the engine off, check the power steering fluid by unscrewing the cap on the pump and looking at the dipstick. With some cars, you can use automatic transmission fluid, but others require special power steering fluid. Look it up in your owner's manual.

>> **Keep a close eye on the brake fluid level in the master cylinder reservoir.**

With a translucent, plastic master cylinder reservoir, you can see the brake fluid level from the outside. You'll have to remove the cover of a metal or opaque plastic reservoir. Keep it nearly full. Many master cylinder reservoirs have two separate chambers. The fluid level in the one that goes to the front disc brakes will fall as the linings wear out (the pistons in the calipers move outward to take up the space, so more fluid is required to fill the calipers' cylinders). This is normal.

Brake fluid has an affinity for water, and moisture will not only cause corrosion in the hydraulic components and Antilock Brake System (ABS), but can also increase stopping distances if it gets hot enough to boil. So, make sure the reservoir lid is on tightly, and keep the can's cap snug.

The windshield washer fluid level is visible through the side of the translucent plastic reservoir. Don't fill it with plain water because it'll freeze in cold weather, and it doesn't clean nearly as well as washer fluid, which is the cheapest automotive liquid you can buy.

EXTRA: Accidental Paint Remover

Brake fluid is a strong paint remover, so don't drip any on the fender. If you should get some on the paint, or on anything at all for that matter, rinse it off with water immediately.

4. Battery terminals

Corroded or loose battery clamps are probably the most common cause of a no-crank/no-start situation, although a dead battery isn't far behind.

Battery terminals are either two lead posts that stick up out of the top of the battery, or two threaded holes in the side, the style made popular by General Motors. Look for fluffy greenish-white corrosion, and try to twist the clamps that hold the battery cables to the posts to make sure they're tight.

NOTE: *Any time you're dealing with a battery, it's important that you wear safety glasses—SULFURIC ACID is present. Wash your hands, too.*

If you find such corrosion on a top-terminal battery, use a wrench (probably 10 mm on late models, but perhaps a 13 mm or 1/2 inch on older vehicles) to loosen the negative clamp (marked with either Neg or a minus sign), then pry it open at its seam with a wide-blade screwdriver, and lift the clamp off the terminal. Or, use a puller made for the purpose, which is an inexpensive tool. Then, do the same with the positive cable. By the way, you'll lose the preset stations in your radio in the process (see #93, page 156).

>> **Clean and tighten the battery terminals and the cable clamps periodically.**

>> **Side terminals require a 5/16-inch wrench.**

You can use a rag and whatever type of spray cleaner you might have handy to get rid of all that white stuff, but a better way to do it is to make a strong solution of baking soda and water (several tablespoons of the former with maybe a cup of the latter) and brush it over the top of the battery, then rinse with plain water.

To make sure you've got good, clean connections, you can use an inexpensive tool available just about everywhere that shaves the old lead off the terminals and the inside of the clamps. Or, just use whatever

sandpaper or emery paper you might have around. You want to see shiny metal. Install the clamps and tighten the nuts, and your problem will probably disappear. Unless, that is, the battery itself is beyond its useful life.

GM-style side-terminal batteries are much less prone to terminal corrosion, but you should still clean the connections. Using a 5/16-inch wrench, unscrew the negative cable first, then the positive. Remove any corrosion you find, then re-install.

5. Accessory drive belts

Most of the cars on the road today use a single "serpentine" belt to power accessories off the engine's crankshaft. These belts are flat with numerous V grooves in the inside surface, and are kept at the proper tightness by an automatic, spring-loaded tensioner. Older vehicles may have plain V-belts, which wear faster, but are less expensive to replace.

If a belt snaps, you'll have to stop the car as soon as possible. With the serpentine type, none of your accessories will be working. That means no power steering, no battery charging from the alternator, and, in most cars, no coolant circulation because the water pump will stop, which will result in instant overheating and serious engine damage if you don't shut it down immediately. On some cars, the water pump is driven by the camshaft drive belt, so coolant will still flow, but that still leaves the other problems.

Older models with two or more belts will, obviously, lose the function of whatever accessory is no longer being powered when a belt breaks.

A slipping belt may be worn or contaminated with oil, or

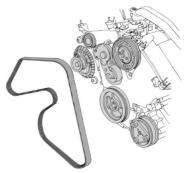

>> **Serpentine belts were a great advance. Make sure to heed the routing diagram.**

29

perhaps it's too loose because of a neglected adjustment or a faulty self-tensioner. Don't go out and buy a spray can of belt dressing. It went out with the introduction of flat micro V-belts, and never really worked on old-fashioned V-belts anyway. The real fix is to replace the belt, and perhaps the spring-loaded idler pulley that maintains proper tension. On the non-self-tensioning belts, whether V or flat multi-V, adjust the tightness as necessary to prevent slipping. This is commonly done by means of a jack screw, a 1/2-inch-drive ratchet in a square hole in the idler pulley bracket. Or, simply prying one of the pivoted components, such as the alternator, tightly against the belt, using a lever, then tighten the lock bolt.

6. Radiator hoses

The big hoses that run from the radiator (always located at the very front of the engine compartment) to the engine are an important maintenance item, and a frequent cause of coolant leaks and overheating breakdowns. They may actually last a long time, but conventional wisdom says they should be replaced every four years. They tend to deteriorate at their connections, and the

›› Radiator hoses deteriorate like this internally.

rubber will feel very soft before they blow.

Replacement should be done when the engine is absolutely cold.

7. Radiator

Radiator repair used to be a big business. No more. Modern radiators just seem to last and last, which is due not only to the materials used, but also to better antifreeze recipes that reduce corrosion and erosion. When they do eventually fail, say by leaking at the gaskets between the tanks and the core, or from the core itself due to physical damage, or by becoming clogged from poor maintenance, the trend is to replace them with a whole new unit instead of repairing them.

8. Air filter and ducts

The air-filter element is composed of a porous, fluffy, paperlike material pleated to give lots of surface area through which the engine breathes. As this becomes clogged with dust, dirt, pollen, insects, and so forth, it begins to restrict the flow of air. If clogging gets bad enough, it can actually reduce engine performance.

Replacement is typically recommended every 30,000

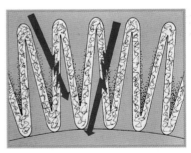

>> **The porous air-filter element keeps dirt, dust, pollen, and other things out of the engine.**

miles. On older cars with carburetors or throttle-body injection, the air cleaner is right on top of the engine, so this is easy. Simply unscrew the wing nut that holds the lid of the air-cleaner housing down, take off the lid, remove the old filter element, wipe out the housing, and install the new element.

Later models have a plastic air-cleaner box tucked into the side of the engine compartment, so they connect to the engine's intake by means of a large-diameter duct. Sometimes it's difficult to unsnap the clips or remove the screws that hold the top of the box on, but otherwise the replacement procedure is the same as that above.

EXTRA: MAF Duct Integrity

>> **If this duct develops a rip or crack it will upset the engine management system.**

Be careful with this duct. If it should become torn, punctured, or disconnected, not only will it admit unfiltered air, thus causing accelerated internal engine wear, but on later models with a Mass Air Flow (MAF) sensor mounted at or near the lid of the air-cleaner box, the PCM (Powertrain Control Module—the engine management computer) will get inaccurate input on the volume of air the engine is ingesting, so will make poor decisions. In other words, the engine will run badly, and the Malfunction Indicator Lamp (MIL) will probably go on to boot.

Breakdowns

Management and Safety Strategies

9. The car is your safe haven

A motor vehicle amounts to a pretty solid and safe environment. Inside, you won't be run over by another car, fall into a hole in the dark, be attacked by a deranged guard dog, get mugged, or slip on the ice. So, if your car quits running, it often makes sense to turn the emergency flashers on, stay inside and wait for help to arrive. This, of course, would be greatly facilitated by the use of a cell phone. Otherwise, you'll have to wait for the next patrol car. You can hang a white rag out the window, or get out long enough to open the hood as an SOS.

10. If you *must* get out...

S uppose you are in a familiar neighborhood, or out in the country where it's not likely that a police car will pass anytime soon. Or, maybe you're just in a hurry. Regardless of the reason, leave your emergency flashers on, take anything valuable with you, lock the car, and start walking. It may be tempting to hitchhike, but there's always the chance that you'll be picked up by an ax murderer.

11. Who to call

If you've been wise enough to establish a solid relationship with a particular service shop, make sure you carry the business card in your glove compartment, because it only makes sense to call that number first. Since you're a regular customer, the shop owner or service advisor will arrange for a tow, or even make a road call. You might break down when the shop's not open, though, or when you're on a trip out of town, so you need additional strategies.

Calling 911 seems a bit excessive for a mere mechanical malfunction, but if you feel you are in any kind of danger, go ahead. Many states offer a more direct alternative for traffic situations—not only accidents, but breakdowns or encounters with drunken or enraged drivers. In Florida, for instance, you can dial *F-H-P (for Florida Highway Patrol, which translates into *3-4-7 on the keypad) and you'll be connected to the nearest FHP station. Other states will, obviously, use their own initials.

Otherwise, find a phone book and look in the yellow pages under "Automobile Repairing & Servicing," or "Towing—Automotive."

If you belong to the Automobile Association of America (AAA) Auto Club, now is definitely the time to use it. Call the 800 number for your region. Do the same for other automotive emergency plans, such as the one from the

American Association of Retired Persons (AARP).

Of course, if your car is covered by a roadside assistance program through the automaker, an emergency is exactly what it's intended for. Call and you'll get a free tow to the nearest dealership service department ASAP.

Won't Go

12. No-crank or no-fire starting failures

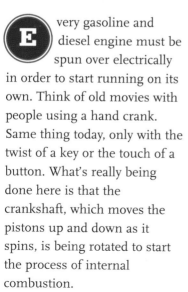

Every gasoline and diesel engine must be spun over electrically in order to start running on its own. Think of old movies with people using a hand crank. Same thing today, only with the twist of a key or the touch of a button. What's really being done here is that the crankshaft, which moves the pistons up and down as it spins, is being rotated to start the process of internal combustion.

Think about how your engine sounds when you get in the car and twist the key. Not the sound of the engine actually running, but before that.

Okay, do you hear that familiar sound (let's say, "chee-chee," or "ruh-ruh")? No? Then you either hear a rapid clicking sound, or nothing at all, and you've got a relatively simple problem. Perhaps the battery has lost its power because you left the lights or some other accessory on, or maybe it's simply gone beyond its useful life (rarely much more than four years). Either way, it should be tested, and, if necessary, replaced.

Other possible causes of a no-crank condition are corroded or loose battery cable clamp connections, and, often overlooked, a bad ground connection between the negative cable and the engine block or cylinder head (ground is the negative side of a direct-current circuit—the whole chassis, engine and body are grounded, as opposed to "hot," which is the positive side).

A no-fire (in other words, the engine won't start running) is the real no-start, and can be much more complicated. The engine will spin over fine when you twist the key, but never catches. The three legs of the internal combustion tripod are fuel, ignition, and compression, and one leg is missing.

If the engine hasn't snapped its timing belt or stripped one

>> If the engine won't start, one way to check for the presence of high voltage is with a simple spark tester.

of its timing chain sprockets so that the camshaft isn't turning, or blown a cylinder head gasket, chances are the compression part is okay. So, try to differentiate between lack of fuel and lack of ignition spark. The easiest way to do this is to spray a tiny amount of starting fluid (previously known as "ether"—it comes in aerosol cans) into the air-intake duct, then crank the engine. If the engine starts momentarily, then dies, you'll know you've got spark, but no fuel. If it just cranks and shows no evidence of firing, there's no spark.

Another way to check for lack of ignition is with a spark tester. Pull a spark plug wire off a plug (grab the boot that goes around the plug, not the wire itself, and give a twist before pulling), connect it to the tester, then ground the tester to the engine (it has a clip for that purpose). Now, have a helper try to start the engine while you watch the tester. If you don't see a robust spark, the problem is in the ignition system.

Driving through deep puddles can drown an ignition system, causing the high voltage to go to ground before it reaches the spark plugs. You may be able to get going again by drying off the distributor and spark plug wires, removing the distributor cap and soaking up any water you find inside, then spraying everything with a water-displacing, multipurpose oil, such as WD-40. Unfortunately, once this kind of high-voltage escape has occurred, it will probably leave carbon tracks on or in the distributor cap, which will cause a miss (rough running). A new cap and rotor will rectify the situation.

In a case where you've determined that a lack of fuel is the trouble, the first thing to do is check the fuse for the fuel pump (there's gas in the tank, right?). You can find its location in your owner's manual. Also, some cars, such as many Ford models, have an inertia switch that's supposed to break the fuel pump circuit when it senses the impact of an accident. Sometimes, however, just a little shock such as bumping into a snow bank or a curb can trip it. Once again, find out how to reset the inertia switch in your owner's manual.

Beyond that, you'll have to consult the specific trouble-shooting information for your car, or have it towed to a professional.

>> **When jump-starting, follow the proper procedure to keep from igniting the hydrogen gas that all car batteries generate.**

13. Jump-starting

If your battery runs down so that the engine won't crank over fast enough to start—you'll hear either a slow groaning noise, or repeated clicking from the starter solenoid—you can usually use jumper cables to get it running. Once you've found a volunteer to help you, park his or her car nose-to-nose with or alongside of yours, and raise both hoods. With one cable, connect the positive post of your car's battery (there'll be a plus sign or "Pos" written on the battery case) to the positive post of the other car.

Using the other cable, connect the negative post of the donor car to a heavy bolt or metal bracket on your engine some distance from the battery. Don't attach it to your negative battery post because if a spark occurs it could ignite the hydrogen that's always hanging around over the battery. Do you remember the Hindenburg? Same gas, same danger of explosion. Also, never allow the two cable clamps to touch or you'll get a big spark and the clamps may try to weld themselves together.

Start the donor car and let it run for at least five minutes, preferably longer. This will give your battery an initial charge. With the donor car running at fast idle, start your engine, then disconnect the cables, negative (or ground) first.

14. Charging a battery

If your vehicle's battery is reasonably new, but has been run down because of leaving the lights or some other accessory on without the engine running (that is, without the alternator replenishing the charge), you will probably be able to get rolling again by means of a battery charger. This device

>> **It's a slow process, but a battery charger will replenish the electrical potential in those cells.**

plugs into a wall socket and has two wires that clip to the battery terminals. It steps household voltage down to something over 12 volts, and charges your car's battery, usually at a rate of between 3 and 10 amperes per hour.

While a full, solid charge will take a day or so with a typical do-it-yourselfer-level charger, you can usually put enough of what's called a "surface charge" on the battery's plates in a few hours or less, and that'll probably get you started. From there on, the alternator takes over the task.

15. Installing a new battery

In cases where your battery goes dead again (no or slow cranking), or if it has failed a capacity or voltage test, or if it's over four years old and has left you stranded one too many times, you need a new one. If you don't want to have an independent repair shop, a mass merchandiser, a tire store, a dealership service department, or some other service facility install it, you can do it yourself. Just be aware that (a) a battery is a heavy component that'll require some muscle on your part, and, (b) you'll need some tools.

First, use a wrench of the proper size to remove the

>> **A bracket may hold down the battery.**

negative battery cable. For the top terminal type, this will usually be 10 mm, 13 mm, or $^1/_2$-inch, but the side-terminal variety found on GM products requires a $^5/_{16}$-inch wrench. Remove the positive cable also.

Now, ascertain what kind of battery hold-down your vehicle uses. Typically, there will be either a bracket that goes across the top of the battery and is anchored to two "J" hooks that stick up through it and are fastened with nuts, or a little wedge that fits into a notch at the bottom of the battery and is held down with a bolt.

Once you've freed the battery, lift it out of the engine compartment. Many batteries have built-on lift straps. If not, you might want to invest in one of the cleverly designed and inexpensive tools that are available to give you a good grip. Be careful of your back! The main internal ingredient of a battery is lead, so this will be a heavy object no matter how small the car.

Take a good look at the cable clamps and the tray that holds the battery. You should take this opportunity to clean up any evidence of corrosion, especially the powdery white kind. It's traditional to use a solution of baking soda and water applied with a brush to eliminate this, but any kind of household spray cleaner will work pretty well. Rinse with clean water. If the battery tray is made of steel, you might want to spray it with undercoating, or a primer paint that soaks into rust.

Install the cable clamps, positive side first, being careful not to let your wrench bridge the terminals—or you'll get a big spark that can melt the wrench. Tighten them, and it wouldn't hurt to coat the clamps with a special spray that keeps corrosion at bay. Or, you can install those little felt washers that are impregnated with oil.

16. Sudden stop

Suppose you're driving and the engine just suddenly goes dead. Your first order of business, of course, is to coast off the road to get as far from the danger of being rear-ended as possible.

Once you're stopped in a safe place, you've got to decide whether this is something you can fix yourself, or if you need to call for a tow.

The usual causes of a sudden loss of motive power are (a) running out of gas, (b) a clogged fuel filter, (c) a blown electric fuel pump fuse, or some other problem with the fuel pump circuit, (d) an ignition system failure, (e) a snapped Overhead Camshaft (OHC) drive belt, or, heaven forbid, (f) a ruptured cylinder head gasket, a thrown connecting rod, a broken crankshaft, or other internal engine catastrophe.

While you can easily take care of getting some gasoline (in an ANSI/ASTM-approved container, of course) and pouring it into the tank, or replacing the fuel pump fuse, it would require a truly dedicated do-it-yourselfer to tackle any of the others. So, in most cases it's time to have the car towed to a repair facility.

17. No power to the wheels

Suppose the engine starts, runs, and revs, but you can't get the car to move. With an automatic transmission, the best you can hope for is that the shift linkage has somehow become unhinged. Or, perhaps a leak has robbed the transmission of the fluid it needs to do its job. These are relatively simple problems that can be fixed by adding sufficient fluid to bring the level up to the "Full" mark on the transmission dipstick (probably many quarts), or by repairing the linkage.

If there's an internal transmission problem, on the other hand, you're in for an expensive repair.

If your car has a manual transmission and it grinds when you depress the clutch pedal and try to put it into first gear, you've probably got a clutch linkage problem. This mechanism may be a mechanical affair using levers and pushrods if it's an old car, or, more likely, a cable or a hydraulic system. Regardless, it's not disengaging the clutch and a professional repair is necessary. If you can put the transmission into gear, but nothing happens when you let the clutch out, the clutch itself is either worn out, broken, or jammed. Again, this will require a major repair job, which includes removing the transmission.

EXTRA: Shop Around

Don't just have your transmission fixed anywhere. Shop around. If your regular automotive service provider doesn't do transmissions, ask the proprietor to recommend someone. This is a highly specialized area of repair, so you've got to find somebody who knows the fine points. Also, see if you can get a nationwide warranty on the repair. That's important if you travel out of state.

Flat Tire
18. Spares

>> **A full-size spare should be included in your tire rotation program.**

Full-size
A full-size spare tire is just what its name implies: the same size as the other four tires that support your vehicle. It should be included in your tire rotation schedule. (You do rotate to get maximum tread life, don't you?)

Compact
The compact spare gave car designers new and welcomed freedom. The large amount of space and weight required to carry around a full-size spare was dramatically reduced. The drawback is that you're not supposed to run these little, high-pressure tires at more than 50 mph, and they're not designed to last for long

>> **Compact spares are supposed to run at high pressures and low speeds.**

distances. Plus, they look ridiculous.

Spare-in-a-can

Here, the auto designers really got the upper hand. All they had to make space for was a pressurized can containing a suitable gas and a sealant intended to plug small holes and seal the area around, say, a nail.

Well, fine, except that tires are sometimes ripped to shreds, or their beads forced from the rims, and no amount of sealant could possibly make them hold pressure again. You're in for a tow.

19. Don't get squashed! Safe changing procedures

Before we go any further on the topic of flat tires, we want to emphasize that a falling car can be lethal. It's not unusual to hear of horrible injuries or death ensuing when a vehicle isn't properly supported during a wheel/tire removal.

Don't fool around with this. A cavalier attitude here can result in tragedy. Do it right:

• Find a level spot well out of the way of traffic. You can't put yourself in a much more dangerous position than sticking your posterior out into the road while you squat to change a tire. If finding a suitable location requires limping along on a flat for a considerable distance and

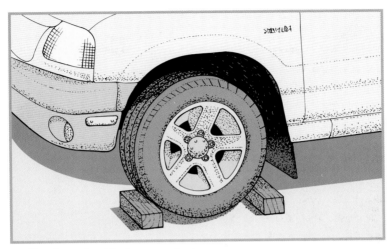

>> **Chock a wheel before you jack.**

possibly ruining that expensive tire and rim, so be it. It'll still be cheaper than hospital or funeral bills. The "level" part is important, too. You don't want to risk the car falling off its jack.

- Since the jack will sink into soft ground, always perform a tire change on pavement. The only exception is if you've had the foresight to carry a one-foot-square or larger piece of 3/4-inch-thick plywood with you, which can serve as a solid base for the jack.

- Putting the transmission in Park and firmly setting the parking brake isn't good enough. You must wedge some kind of chocks tightly in front and in back of at least one tire that's not going to be raised off the ground. It would be sensible to carry the actual items (collapsible chocks are available) with you, but failing in that you can use chunks of 2 x 4, or even any substantial rocks you find lying around. Just use something, or there's a chance the car will roll off the jack, certainly damaging itself and possibly injuring you.

• Never, ever, place your hand, foot, or head under any part of the suspension, brakes, or chassis while the wheel is off.

Get out your owner's manual and read the appropriate section. This will not only make things go more smoothly, but may prevent you from damaging the car by jacking at the wrong spot. Another thing that will be

explained is antitheft wheel locks, if you happen to have them.

Once you're satisfied that the car isn't going to roll anywhere, use the lug wrench to try to loosen the wheel lugs. This may require you to pop off a wheel cover or a hubcap, or to remove decorative plastic caps that look like nuts. On almost all vehicles out there today, the lugs unscrew in the "normal" direction—in other words, counterclockwise. There are some exceptions among older cars, but the end of the stud will probably be marked with

>> **Some lug nuts have plastic covers for decoration.**

>> **The stock lug wrench might work if the studs aren't corroded and if nobody overtightened the nuts.**

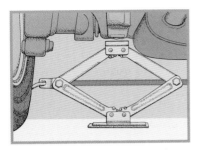

>> Look up jack placement in your owner's manual for safety and to prevent damage to the car.

an "L" (for "left-hand," referring to the tightening direction) to tip you off.

Decide which you're more comfortable with: pressing down, or pulling up. Then, put the hex of the lug wrench over the nut and apply force. If you can't budge it by pressing down, try the opposite. If it's still not working, you need more leverage. You can put a piece of pipe over the factory lug wrench. (Remember Archimedes?) An X-type lug wrench would be a good addition to your complement of on-board tools. Regardless of what you use, just break them loose. Don't remove them yet.

Once the lugs are broken loose, you can jack up the car. Go far enough so that the flat tire is well off the ground or the spare may not fit in the space. Unscrew the lugs and remove the wheel/tire assembly. Put the spare on—it might take a couple of tries to get the studs lined up with the holes—and thread all the lugs on hand-tight. Lower the car, then tighten the lugs as much as you can with the wrench. With the common five-lug design, do this in a star pattern (think of drawing a star on paper—always go to the opposite side from the one you've just done). On four-lug wheels, go across. Just never go right around as it can cause the brake disc to warp.

20. Inflators

>> **A spare-in-a-can will usually get you rolling if the tire has a puncture or a bead leak.**

Of course, you may not be physically up to the whole procedure of changing a tire, or maybe the weather's too bad or you're too well dressed. There is an alternative to calling a tow truck that may work well enough to get you to a tire repair shop: an aerosol inflator. These contain a liquid sealant that can fill small punctures, and sufficient compressed gas to inflate the tire enough to allow you to drive at least a short distance. These are handy and inexpensive, so you may want to carry one with you. Then, when you get a flat from something like a nail (which will probably still be in there), just shake the can, screw it to the tire valve, and inflate until the can is empty. You may find the leak in the process because you'll probably see a foamy white substance (the sealant) bubbling out of the tread somewhere.

21. Practice ahead of time

Pretty much everybody has a flat at some time or other, so if you want to reduce the stress and danger involved in putting on the spare why not do a dry run ahead of time? Besides the dress rehearsal, you'll have the opportunity to free up any lugs that have been overtightened or are seized from corrosion (just soak them with an all-purpose oil).

Leaks
22. Coolant (antifreeze)

A mixture of water and antifreeze (ideally, 50 percent each) is the medium that carries waste heat out of your engine and dissipates it to the atmosphere (via the radiator). If this function were to cease, that expensive assembly would melt down into a worthless lump of scrap metal in short order. Not that long ago, all antifreeze was a green or greenish-gold color, but today it may be orange, yellow, pink, amber, red, or blue instead. It also has a characteristic odor that defies our powers of description. Burnt sugar? Not quite.

The most common cooling-system leaks occur at the connection points of the rubber hoses that route the liquid to and from the radiator (large diameter) and the heater core (smaller diameter). You'll probably smell them long before you see puddles in the driveway, or you'll see steam wafting out

>> Most radiator hose leaks occur at the connections.

from the hood seam. Open the hood and look around using a good light. Leaks will show up as accumulations of the colored antifreeze, and, of course, as wetness.

The rubber companies that make radiator and heater hoses want you to replace them every four years to avoid the possibility of a catastrophic breakdown. We've seen them last much longer than that, but the manufacturers have a point because a severe overheating event can ruin a multi–thousand dollar engine.

Coolant leaks can and do occur elsewhere as well. Although modern Plastic Tank Radiators (PTRs) hold up very well indeed, they do tend to develop leaks at the gaskets between the tanks and the core, and, eventually, in the core itself, from corrosion.

23. Motor oil

T he black spots on the driveway are bad enough, but when oil gets tracked in on the carpet, that takes the situation to another whole level. Oil leaks are messy, especially in the engine compartment and the nether regions thereof where all drips must eventually gather. They are not, however, much of a threat to the durability and dependability of your car. The only leaks we've seen that can become severe enough to make it impossible to keep the oil level up to normal are those at the rear main crankshaft seal. Fortunately, this type isn't very common these days.

When you see evidence of a leak, the first thing to suspect should be the seam between what's variously called the valve cover, rocker cover, or cam

>> **Before you have a repair done for a leaky valve-cover gasket, try tightening the screws, bolts, or nuts.**

cover and the cylinder head. Sometimes this leak can be vastly reduced, or even eliminated, by just tightening the small screws that fasten the cover down. Don't overdo it or

>> **Fluorescent dye added to the crankcase oil will show up under a UV light, thus highlighting a leak's location.**

you'll split the gasket. Screwdriver force should be plenty.

The very best way to find the source of a leak is to put ultraviolet dye in the crankcase, then look at all the seams with a powerful black light (the one that made the Jefferson Airplane poster in your dorm room pop just won't cut it). Do-it-yourselfergrade UV leak-detection kits are available for under $40.

Severe oil leaks should certainly be taken care of for reasons other than general cleanliness. If the liquid lube is keeping some rubber component such as a motor mount saturated, it will eventually dissolve the part. The starter and its wiring, which is often on the receiving end, can also be put out of commission by being bathed in oil.

24. Automatic transmission fluid (ATF)

If you see evidence of this cherry-red hydraulic fluid on your garage floor, possible causes range from the trivial to the profound. If you're lucky, the leak will be at one of the lines or connections that route ATF to and from the fluid cooler in the bottom of the radiator.

Other not-so-bad fluid-escape routes are through the gasket between the transmission/transaxle pan and the case, and, on rear-wheel-drive vehicles, at the seal for the driveshaft yoke.

Beyond those possibilities, you're probably going to have to visit a repair shop (see #17, page 43).

EXTRA: Temporary Fix

If the car isn't worth an expensive repair, you can try one of the transmission sealer additives that are on the market. They swell internal seals and can successfully choke off a leak, but not forever.

25. Power steering fluid

The first symptom of this leak that most people notice is a howling noise when they turn the wheel. That's the power steering pump complaining that it's running dry.

There are several possibilities. First, check the hoses that run from the power steering pump (at the front of the engine, with a pulley driven by the accessory belt) to the steering gear. If the steering gear is of the rack-and-pinion type, it's a long pipe-like affair mounted crosswise near the bottom of the firewall. The recirculating-ball variety found mostly on big, rear-wheel-drive domestic vehicles is a substantial cast-metal box mounted on the driver's-side frame rail—the steering column goes directly into it.

The seals at either end of the pump's shaft tend to leak after long service. Rack-and-

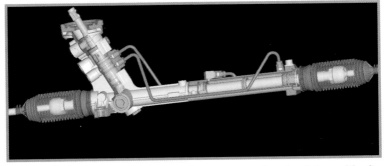

>> **Power rack-and-pinion steering gears may develop internal leaks that cause the boots over the inner tie rod ends to fill with fluid.**

pinion units develop internal leaks eventually, too. Squeeze the rubber boots that keep the dirt out to see if they're full of fluid. Recirculating-ball steering gears also have seals that have been known to fail.

If you're not a stickler about keeping your car right up to snuff, you might want to try a bottle of power steering fluid with a stop-leak additive. It swells old seals and may just stave off repair for a year or so.

While it's possible to replace rack-and-pinion seals, the success rate isn't high, so this problem is usually rectified by the installation of a remanufactured unit.

26. Brake fluid

Here's one you don't want to fool with. Any brake fluid leak is serious business. The vulnerable points in the brake hydraulic system are the flexible rubber hoses that run from the chassis to the wheel brakes, and the rigid metal lines that route fluid pressure to all four corners. The hoses can become chafed or cut, or can just balloon after years of containing all that pressure. The danger with the metal lines is corrosion. We've seen instances of total brake failure when these small-diameter pipes rusted through.

Although leaks in the piston seals of disc brake calipers do occur, they're pretty rare. If your car has rear drum brakes, however, which incorporate a small dual-piston wheel cylinder and curved shoes that press against the inside of a shallow drum, they will surely develop leaks at the wheel cylinder seals sooner or later.

Since there's such a small volume of fluid involved in the whole system, leaks are not usually obvious. In the case of rear drum-brake wheel cylinders (since the early 1970s, found only at the rear), you may see that the inside of the tire is wet and shiny. Otherwise, there may be no evidence. That's why it's so important to keep an eye on the fluid in the master cylinder reservoir. Even without any leaks, the level will fall gradually as the disc brake linings wear (front discs have been used on most cars since the 1970s), but a sudden drop should serve as an alarm—have those brakes inspected thoroughly on a lift.

SOS: Warning Lamps
27. Charging system

I f the warning lamp on the dash—typically labeled "Batt"—flickers while the car is idling, it means that electrical accessories are using more current than the alternator is capable of producing at that speed. In other words, power is being drawn from the battery to make up the shortfall. If the lamp winks out when you rev the engine a little, or while you're driving down the road, the charging system is working.

This may be a case of a loose, worn, wet, or oil-contaminated drivebelt.

If the light goes on and stays on regardless of engine speed, the drive belt is still the first thing to check, but it's likely that the alternator itself (or whatever regulates its field current—this may be a separate voltage regulator, or a function of the engine management computer) has burned out. In the old days, you could drive quite a distance on the battery alone, probably far enough to get service. Today's cars are so thirsty for amperage to run computers, fuel pumps and injectors, and all kinds of accessories, however, that you won't make it far before battery voltage drops below what's needed to keep the circuits alive, and the car will stop dead. If it's dark so that you've got to have the extra electrical draw of the headlights, forget it.

28. Oil pressure

 low reading on a gauge, or a glowing warning light, is serious business. Something's interfering with a critical operation: keeping the engine's internal parts supplied with sufficient oil to maintain the film of molecules that prevents wear.

First, kill the engine and check the oil level with the dipstick. If it's low, use some other form of transportation to go buy several quarts of the proper grade of brand-name oil, and pour enough into the engine to bring the level up to the Full or Max mark on the dipstick.

Okay, what happened? If you've been lax about maintenance and the oil level has dropped too low because you never bother to check it or have it changed, and the light goes out when you start the engine, you've had a close call, and we hope you'll mend your ways.

On the other hand, if the level's okay and the warning light is on, you've got a big problem. Low oil pressure can be caused by worn-out main and rod bearings (replacement is an expensive job), or by a worn or nonfunctioning oil pump (not as big a deal). You'll probably start hearing a bearing knock any day now, and that's the sure and certain precursor of engine destruction.

29. Check engine

>> **The Malfunction Indicator Lamp glows when the On-Board Diagnostic system has detected a problem.**

Whether the carmaker labels it "Check Engine," "Service Engine Soon," or "Power Loss," in the auto repair industry that warning light goes by the acronym MIL (Malfunction Indicator Lamp). That's its generic Society of Automotive Engineers (SAE) name.

An illuminated MIL indicates that the Powertrain Control Module (PCM) has detected a malfunction in the complex network of sensors,

actuators, electronics, etc. that makes the clean-running, good-performing vehicles we have today possible.

This is an important part of the On-Board Diagnostics (OBD) system, the earliest manifestations of which appeared in 1980 or so. By Environmental Protection Agency (EPA) mandate, from 1996 onward every car, SUV, and light truck sold in the U.S. has

>> **The standard OBD II data link connector is usually located to the left of the steering column.**

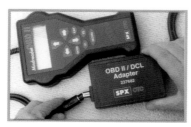

>> **Technicians can access trouble codes and other engine management system information by using a scan tool.**

had the added benefit of OBD II. This very comprehensive system of self-criticism has the capability of performing automatic tests of many things in a vehicle that can affect emissions. The MIL will come on if any of the tests have failed, and, if something deemed especially serious is noticed, such as a frequent misfire, the MIL will blink. It will also light up if

EXTRA: Gas Cap Tight?

About the only thing the average motorist can address when faced with an illuminated MIL is the tightness of the gas cap. A cap left loose at fill-up is probably the most common trigger of this warning. So, the first thing to do is unscrew the cap, then screw it back on tightly. After a length of time determined by what kind of driving you do, the system will run the evaporative emissions test monitor again (one of the self-tests just mentioned), and will turn the light out if a passing grade is achieved.

one of the sensor signals it receives is out of its normal range.

The engine management computer then generates a Diagnostic Trouble Code (DTC), which helps guide the repair technician to the source of the problem. These codes are accessed through a standard 16-pin Data Link Connector (DLC), regardless of the brand of car. The DLC is supposed to be located under the dash to the left of center, although there are exceptions. The technician plugs his scan tool (an expensive, handheld electronic diagnostic device with an LCD screen) into the DLC, then reads any DTCs, and also usually looks at other available data.

30. Brake or ABS lamp

>> **The ABS lamp commonly comes on because of a wheel speed sensor problem.**

On older vehicles not equipped with an Antilock Braking System (ABS), the illumination of the "Brake" light on the dash means either that the parking brake has not been released, or that a leak or air in the brake hydraulic system has caused imbalance in the two circuits. By U.S. law, since 1967, all cars sold in this country must have two separate hydraulic circuits, so that if one blows, some braking capability will be maintained. See if repeatedly applying and releasing the parking brake makes the light go off. If not, it's time for a professional brake inspection.

On vehicles with ABS, the brake warning light (which may be labeled "ABS") usually means that input from one of the wheel-speed sensors isn't right, or has stopped altogether, resulting in the loss of the antilock function. You can drive the car, but remember that you are doing so without benefit of this important safety feature. Get it serviced.

No Fun to Drive?

Not-So-Petty Annoyances
31. Wander

This can make a highway drive a chore instead of a pleasure. It's the tendency of the car to float aimlessly in one direction or the other instead of holding a straight course while cruising along a level road so that you have to make constant small directional corrections.

The causes are, typically, wear in the steering components, or improper

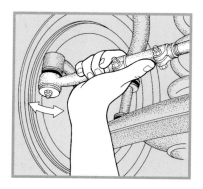

alignment of the front suspension. Wear results in "lash" that allows the wheels to flop from side to side when varying pavement conditions are encountered. The suspects are the inner socket assemblies of rack-and-pinion steering gears, tie-rod ends, and the idler or pitman arms of traditional recirculating-ball steering-gear systems, as will be found on many big domestic rear-wheel-drive (RWD) vehicles, such as full-size sedans, pickups, and vans.

Direct observation is the best way to find the cause of wander, but you'll need a helper. With the weight on the wheels (in other words, not with the car jacked up by the chassis), have him or her unlock the steering column, then rock the wheel vigorously back and forth while you stick your head underneath and look around, using a good light. With traditional parallelogram linkage, you may see the idler or pitman arm moving up and down, lash in the tie-rod ends, or perhaps more rotational action going into the steering box than coming out. On rack-and-pinion steering, pay special attention to the inner tie-rod ends, and make sure the rack housing itself is firmly mounted. Sure, there's some lash even in a new system, but you should be able to judge excessive wear.

Also, recirculating-ball-type steering gears wear internally, so they have what's known as an "over-center" adjustment that will bring back the original clearances. It's pretty easy to perform this adjustment (all you have to do is loosen the locknut and screw in the threaded bolt that sticks out of the top of the steering gear), but there's always the danger of overdoing it, which can result in a dangerous binding

EXTRA: If the Steering Wheel's Not Straight...

Crooked steering wheels can be related to wandering. Whether recirculating-ball or rack-and-pinion, steering boxes usually have a high point at the straight-ahead position that adds drag to help keep the wheel stationary while cruising the highway. If somebody has tried to get the steering wheel visually straight by repositioning it on its shaft, this design feature will be defeated.

condition. Better leave it to a professional.

Lash may also exist in the joints that allow the steering column to transmit the driver's commands through an angle to the gearbox. The universal joint variety typically lasts and lasts, but the rubberized textile type, fondly known as a "rag joint," often deteriorates to the point that there's excessive play—you can twist the steering wheel quite a bit before there's any action at the steering gear.

Deteriorated upper control-arm bushings can cause serious steering problems, and probably a lot of clunking to boot. Look down on them while your helper holds pressure on the brake pedal and shifts from Drive to Reverse and back. You'll see (and hear) excessive movement.

Alignment really shouldn't change too much over the life of a car. But if it's been tampered with during a repair, or has been thrown off by the impact of striking a curb or a big pothole—which could bend one of those sturdy suspension components—the alignment could end up out of specifications. The setting that affects the ability of a car to stay on a straight path is called "caster," which is the tilt of a wheel's steering axis when viewed from the side. Naturally, this angle should be within specifications. If you've never been satisfied with your car's tendency to stay straight, it is often possible to bias caster more toward the positive direction. You might ask the person who's going to adjust your alignment if adding more caster is a viable option in your case.

32. Pulling to one side

>> **Pulling to one side may be due to nothing more serious than a low tire.**

This situation has to be defined to be conquered. If your car wants to steer to one side or the other instead of going straight on a level road, one set of potential problems presents itself. If, on the other hand, the pull only occurs when you apply the brakes, it's another whole deal.

In the former case, before you start thinking about expensive repairs, make sure the basic vehicle-to-road interface, meaning tires, is okay. Check inflation first. A low tire on one side will tend to make a car pull in that direction. This is because the tire's actual rolling diameter will be smaller than that of its mate on the other side. If you were to look at the car head-on

EXTRA: Pressure Pointing

If the pull is very slight, sometimes you can eliminate it by pumping a few more pounds of air into the front tire on that side than you have in the other, but don't expect dramatic results.

and draw an imaginary line from the top of one tire to the top of the other, then compare it to the road surface, you'd see what amounts to a section of a cone, a geometrical shape that just naturally rolls in a circle. Also, there'll be more tread-to-pavement drag on the low side.

If the problem persists after you've evened up the psi (pounds per square inch), eliminate the possibility that one tire's internal construction gives it a rolling-force bias toward one side by switching the positions of the right and left tire/wheel assemblies. If the car now pulls in the opposite direction of the original symptom, you've found tire trouble. You can swap the fronts to the rear and try again. Or, go shopping for new rubber.

There's more to tires than inflation, namely, tread-wear patterns. For example, if a front tire's tread tends to disappear along the outboard edge, it's likely

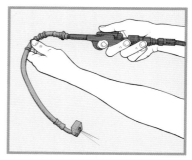

>> **If one front brake hose is clogged, it will cause the vehicle to pull to the opposite side when you hit the brakes.**

that the camber setting (that is, the tilt of the tire/wheel assembly when viewed from the front) at that corner is too positive, and any pull present would probably be toward that side.

If the top of the tire tilts outward, once again you get a cone situation, so the car will tend to pull in that direction. While camber can be checked with a carpenter's level against the rim, the normal thing is to have the car aligned on proper (and expensive) equipment. By the way, crowned roads, to help rain run off, such as found in the country, can certainly make a car steer to the right. So, many old-fashioned alignment technicians dial in an extra bit of positive camber on the left wheel to compensate.

Pulling to one side when the brakes are applied means the stopping power of one front-disc brake caliper isn't the same as that of the other. One common cause is a restricted brake hose that keeps the hydraulic pressure in one caliper from rising as rapidly as it does in the other. Or, perhaps a caliper piston is seized from corrosion so that it can't force the friction material on the brake pad against the disc. In either case, the pull will be toward the opposite side where the brake is actually working. Other possibilities are brake linings that are contaminated with brake fluid, or perhaps grease from the steering linkage, or totally worn out so that just their steel backing plates are contacting the rotor.

Regardless of the cause, this is indicative of a serious brake problem. Also, it can easily induce a skid in slippery conditions. Get it fixed now.

33. Bad vibes

Unpleasant vibrations encountered at highway speeds are commonly due to tire imbalance. You may have noticed those little weights on your rims. They're strategically placed to counter the imperfections in the tires.

There's no practical way for you to restore perfect balance without an expensive machine made for the purpose, so this is another case where you'll have to visit a professional.

If your car is rear wheel drive, it has a long driveshaft under the body that connects the

>> **Small lead weights on the tire rim compensate for inevitable imperfections.**

transmission to the rear axle. To allow the axle to rise and fall as you encounter bumps, the driveshaft has something called a universal joint at either end. When the needle bearings inside a "U" joint wear out, the driveshaft will no longer spin truly, which will cause heavy vibration. It's different from tire imbalance in that it usually is felt at lower speeds, and sometimes it's especially noticeable when you're coming to a stop.

34. Bouncing and leaning

After you hit a bump, does it seem as if you've discovered perpetual motion because your car just keeps bouncing up and down? Or, does your vehicle lean alarmingly when you encounter a tight curve? Either way, the likely culprit is worn-out shock absorbers or struts.

The term "shock absorber" is a misnomer we're stuck with. The springs actually absorb the shock of a bump, then this energy is dissipated through the shock absorber (which is called a strut if it has a coil spring fastened to it). Regardless, it does its job of taming undulations by forcing

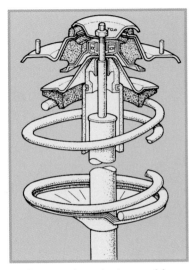

>> **Suspension struts combine the hydraulic damper element (same function as a shock absorber) with the coil spring.**

fluid through various orifices and springloaded valves.

Eventually, the internal parts wear out and you'll notice your car bobbing and leaning, and perhaps taking a nosedive when you hit the brakes hard.

Replacing ordinary shock absorbers would be an easy job except that the nuts and bolts that hold them on are invariably rusted to the point that you may have to chisel or saw them off. Installing new hydraulic inserts in struts requires skill and a special spring compressor.

35. Brake pulsation

C onsidered almost a plague in the auto service business, pulsating brake pedals certainly make driving unpleasant. What's happening with disc brakes is that uneven thickness of the brake discs (also called "rotors") is causing force to be

transmitted through the incompressible hydraulic column in the brake lines back up to the brake pedal. In other words, the "fat" spots on the discs force the "pads" (the friction elements, which are composed of metal plates bonded or riveted to a layer of

>> **If the brake disc wobbles, or has variations in thickness, expect brake-pedal pulsation.**

friction material) back each time they pass through them, and this accounts for the bumpy feeling.

Short of having the rotors machined on a lathe, or replacing them, there's nothing that can be done to eliminate this annoyance. The chances of it occurring, however, could be reduced if everybody in auto service used a torque wrench in the proper tightening pattern when installing wheels, instead of just blasting them on with an air-impact wrench, which can cause the rotor wobble that results in uneven disc wear. So, if you've just had a tire replaced, rebalancing of the wheels done, or a flat changed, this is a likely cause of pulsation.

On cars that have drum brakes at the rear, pulsation, or "hitching," is caused by drums that are out of round. Applying the parking brake (which engages the rears) while coasting will let you know if the problem is with the front discs or the rear drums. Machining or replacement is the cure.

36. Rough idle

If you're mechanically inclined, very little is more annoying than a rough idle. It makes an otherwise fine car seem like a wreck. It's usually caused by one or more cylinders not firing (missing).

The traditional way to isolate which cylinder is not doing its job is to remove one spark plug wire at a time. Use an insulated tool made for the purpose, or you'll get a horrific shock of 10,000 to 50,000 volts. And don't do this on 1996 and up cars with OBD II as it will set a misfire code and illuminate the Malfunction Indicator Lamp (MIL) on the dash. Chances are you'll find one that doesn't make a difference in the smoothness of the idle. Then, you remove that spark plug to see if it's okay, check the spark plug wire for continuity with an ohmmeter,

and perform a compression test using a special gauge that screws into the spark plug hole to find out if the valves are sealing properly. You can replace a spark plug or its wire quite easily, but a burned valve will require major surgery and a formidable set of skills.

Another possible cause of roughness is a vacuum leak in an individual intake manifold runner, which can admit enough extra air to cause a misfire. Also, a fuel injector may be clogged or electrically faulty.

〉〉 On older cars, pull one spark plug wire at a time at idle to find out which cylinder isn't firing.

EXTRA: Limp-In Mode

If the Malfunction Indicator Lamp (MIL) on the dash is illuminated, the Powertrain Control Module (PCM) may have reverted to what is called "limited operating strategy," or "limp-in mode." It will get you home, but performance will be poor. Finding out what caused the MIL to come on requires the highest level of diagnostic skill that a professional auto-repair technician can muster, so we won't waste space on it here.

37. Sluggish performance

Sluggish performance typically develops so gradually that when you finally have it fixed, you'll be pleasantly surprised. Unless your vehicle has a huge number of miles on it, or hasn't been treated to regular oil changes, chances are the internal engine parts are still capable of generating the compression necessary for good performance. So, the most likely cause of poor power is something amiss in the electronic engine management system, which most cars have had since the early 1980s.

>> **The oxygen sensor is the linchpin of the computerized engine management system.**

Another possibility is a lazy oxygen (O_2) sensor. This device reports back to the PCM on the state of the air/fuel ratio by means of rapidly varying voltage. We've always been amazed that they last for any length of time at all since they're screwed into the exhaust system where they're exposed to hot, corrosive gases, but the fact is that they commonly survive for over 100,000 miles.

Not always, though. If an O_2 sensor becomes contaminated, the signal it sends out will be slower in its variations than it should be, but may not be so far off that the PCM recognizes a problem and illuminates the MIL. The faulty signal can reduce performance, so replacing the oxygen sensor may just do the trick. We should mention that all 1996 and up models use two O_2 sensors per catalytic converter, one upstream and one downstream of the "cat" (this is one of the requirements of OBD II—see #29, page 59–60). We're talking about the upstream sensor. In other words, the one closest to the cylinder head.

Most late models have a knock sensor, which can have an effect on horsepower production (see #92, page 155.)

There's one more factor: Weight. Perhaps you're carrying your famous collection of antique anvils in the trunk. Or, maybe just a whole bunch of tools. Regardless, lightening the load will improve performance.

Noises

38. Pad wear indicator

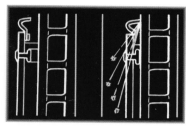

>> **Pad wear indicators can keep you from ruining your brake discs.**

If you hear a high-pitched squeal when you're coasting and just lightly touch the brake pedal, chances are you're getting fair warning that your disc brake linings are worn out. That is, the friction material that's pressed against the disc to stop the car (with its steel backing plate, the assembly is called a pad). The squealing comes from a pad wear indicator. An ingenious device, it's just a simple steel tab that's attached to the pad and contacts the disc when the lining gets too thin, thus signaling that it's time for a brake job. A variation on this theme is a pad with an electrical contact embedded in the lining at a certain depth. When the friction material wears enough to allow the contact to touch the disc, it completes a circuit and lights a lamp on the dash. Heed the warning or you may need to buy new discs along with new pads. Modern discs are relatively thin and light compared to those of the past, however, so replacement is becoming much more common than it once was.

39. Clunks and thumps

T hese noises can be pretty scary to the layman, who's probably expecting something in the underpinnings to give way at any moment when he or she hears unwanted sounds coming from down under. For exhaust systems rattles, see #96, pg. 166.

While such sounds shouldn't be ignored, they are usually not a sign of impending disaster. We're talking about the clunks and thumps you hear when going over a bumpy road, or turning into a driveway. Usually, they're due to a deteriorated rubber bushing, such as might be found on the stabilizer bar links, or a shock absorber mount. Or, they can be from something even easier to fix: a loose suspension-strut gland nut that lets the hydraulic insert bang up and down inside its housing.

Ball joints, which would be dangerous to ignore, usually don't make any noise before they break. You've probably heard of accidents caused by a car's suspension components suddenly letting go. You may even have seen a vehicle lying flat on its belly with a broken ball joint and one of its front wheels at a scary angle. That's not going to happen to you, right? You've always been vigilant.

If your car has lots of miles on it, or even if it hasn't, but is getting old, don't be surprised if some portion of the heavy metal that supports it over terra firma starts complaining. Unfortunately, finding the cause of the noise isn't so easy. The dynamics of a rolling vehicle, the complex nature of modern suspensions, and the way sounds can be telegraphed through the chassis and body make it hard to pinpoint the location of the problem.

If you hear a clunk when the suspension works over bumps, the probable cause is excessive clearance in a joint due to wear. It might be as simple as a loose strut gland nut, or something more subtle, such as a shrunken, dried-out rubber bushing.

As a first step, consult whatever service literature you have available (maybe you can get your friendly local repair shop or dealer to do a search for you as a favor) to see if you can find a Technical Service Bulletin (TSB) that pertains to the noise. Apparently, this is an area where numerous problems show up in the field because it generates quite a few bulletins. Some of these alert you to redesigned replacement parts, while others say the noise is simply a

characteristic of the vehicle and should be accepted as normal.

If no clues are forthcoming, it's time to go hands-on. It'll be helpful if you can get a friend, preferably a hefty one, to assist. For front-end noises, pop the hood, have your comrade press down on the bumper or fender, then release and lift repeatedly until the suspension is really working. Meanwhile, listen carefully and use a good light to examine the upper strut or shock mounts and the control arm joints. If you hear anything untoward, but can't pinpoint the source, place a broomstick against your ear and touch the end to suspected areas. This works almost as well as a mechanic's stethoscope. Nothing obvious? Then lie down and look underneath with your light, even though your friend's stamina may be taxed by this time.

The "dry park check," which will uncover "lash" (meaning

unwanted play) in the steering mechanism, is less physically challenging. Have your helper sit in the driver's seat, turn the key to On to unlock the column, then rock the steering wheel vigorously from side to side while you watch the steering components. There should be next to no visible lash.

By the way, if you raise the car by the frame, suspension and steering parts will be hanging at an unnatural angle, which may mask the looseness you're looking for. So, place your jack and jack stands under the control arms or the rear axle to keep the weight on the suspension components.

Upper A-frame or control arm bushings can be made to disclose their shortcomings by having a helper hold the brakes down firmly, with the engine idling, while shifting from Drive through Neutral to Reverse repeatedly while you look down over the fender.

Some vehicles have substantial horizontal struts that position the lower control arms fore and aft. These are mounted in large rubber bushings, and any clearance here will make itself heard. Also, their mounting points on the frame have been known to rust away, but this causes steering symptoms far more noticeable and worrisome than a mere noise.

Rear-wheel-drive (RWD) vehicles with a live rear axle and coil springs may have what's called a "Panhard rod" that runs diagonally from the chassis to one side of the axle housing. Its bushings are a likely source of clunking.

Worn-out shocks or struts are common culprits here. When the internal hydraulics degrade, the piston will move without the proper resistance, then stop short with a bump. With shocks, another thing to check for is loose or dried-out mounting bushings.

That husky stabilizer bar, the part that helps keep a car level in a curve, is often the source of noise. The links that attach it to the chassis have bushings at both ends, and there is more vulnerable rubber in its mounts.

Of course, some noises that emanate from under a car don't have anything to do with the suspension or steering systems, but it can be difficult to make the distinction. For instance, a broken motor mount can cause a solid thump. Oil soaking may have made it delaminate, or perhaps a couple of bolts have come loose. This sound will be sensitive to getting on or off the throttle, however, not to bumps.

40. Tapping/ knocking

Differentiating between these two sounds is important since one is relatively inexpensive to eliminate, while the other would be very costly indeed.

A tapping, clicking noise coming from the engine is usually due to excessive clearance in the mechanism that opens the valves (some late models still have manually adjustable valves). Or, to oil starvation, which allows hydraulic valve lifters to collapse—check the oil level immediately.

Knocking is called that because it sounds like knuckles rapping on a wooden door. It's a much deeper, "heavier" sound than tapping. Usually, this is caused by worn-out connecting rod bearings, the replacement of which is a pretty big job that can easily escalate into the stratosphere if the crankshaft is damaged, so that the engine has to be removed to do the repair. Or, knocking can be due to a loose piston pin (aka wrist pin), which would also require a major operation, including removing the cylinder head.

Even professionals have difficulty telling bearing knock from piston-pin knock, but it doesn't matter because the oil pan has to come off in either case. The bearings are then inspected directly, and if they're okay, a wrist-pin problem is indicated.

Regardless, if you hear a knock, better stop driving right now because your engine's about to blow. It'll be a lot cheaper to fix if you have it done before there's further damage.

41. Rattles and buzzes

Interior noises can drive you crazy, but with a little help you should be able to find them. First, look around under the seats, in the glove compartment, and elsewhere to see what extraneous stuff you might be carrying around. A high percentage of rattles are caused by junk that shouldn't be in the car in the first place, or by tools that aren't properly stowed.

Speaking of loose cargo: are the jack, lug wrench, and spare properly secured? This would be especially noticeable in vans and SUVs. It can take a while to figure out what that diagram inside the jack compartment cover is trying to tell you to do, but it's worth the time required.

To find the source of the noise, go hands-on. Have

>> Be sure the jack is stowed according to the illustration to avoid rattles.

>> Push on panels and trim while somebody else drives to isolate rattles and buzzes.

somebody else drive while you press on panels, doors, windows, handles, trim, and so on until you find that the sound changes. Sometimes this will require quite a push, especially if you suspect the dashboard or a door panel.

Glove compartment and console doors typically close against little rubber bumpers. Is one missing? Do they look dried out and shrunken? Or, how

about the window channels? Are they worn out? Gone altogether? Also, look for missing screws.

Once you think you've found the problem, try wedging cardboard or a wooden tongue depressor between the offending components to tighten them up. If the noise disappears, you'll know your job is to duplicate what the spacer is doing.

Latches for, say, the glove compartment or console lid can usually be adjusted. This may require a Phillips screwdriver, an Allen wrench, or a Torx bit. Move the catch in the direction that

>> Adjust the console and glove box latches to eliminate annoying noises.

makes the fit as tight as possible while still being lockable.

Sometimes, the unoccupied passenger seat will produce a rattle that's downright thunderous. What's the problem? Too much space in the tracks. You can usually fix this by taking up the clearance. Loosen the bolts that hold the tracks down, then spread them as far as you can and retighten. This can do wonders.

Tailgates, whether of a pickup or of certain truck-based SUVs, can sound like a handful of bolts in a cement mixer. One thing that typically happens is that the rubber rings on the hinged arms that keep the tailgate from falling away dry out, or break and are lost. Then, the heavy steel arms hit both the body and the gate. Replace the rubber, or in some

EXTRA: Are Your Sunglasses Buzzing?

Those overhead storage compartments for glasses, garage door openers, and so forth are sure convenient, but they're made of hard plastic and are likely to generate an excruciating buzz. Unfortunately, the catches aren't adjustable. Press various portions while driving to isolate the offending seam, then cut and glue in foam strips of a suitable thickness to make the mating tight.

cases, where available, substitute rubber-coated cables for the hinged arms.

Hatches of minivans, SUVs, or hatchbacks can be noisy. They're big parts of the vehicle structure and just naturally generate sounds as the body twists and bends. Open it and take a look. Are there rubber wedges intended to impede movement? What kind of shape are they in? In some cases, improved parts are available that compensate for a design problem.

The sliding doors of vans also can make big noises. Since many versions use steel rollers riding on steel tracks, the potential for trouble is obvious. Try to take up excess clearance by loosening the roller bracket bolts, then moving the bracket down. In some cases, you can get replacement rollers made of nylon or Hytrel™.

Whether you smoke or not, you've got an ashtray, and this mechanism can be complex.

Sometimes the fabric strips that prevent metal-to-metal or plastic-to-plastic contact wear out or are lost. Also, the little rubber bumper stops may be missing or flattened.

A license plate bracket, although outside the car, may cause a rattle you can hear inside. Remove the plate and look for stripped or corroded mounting screws. Substitute fasteners of a larger diameter, but make sure they've got an anticorrosion plating.

What materials make sense for insulating one component from another? Whatever will fit easily and stand up to the environment (plenty of heat and UV from the sun). You need some dense foam rubber—a piece of an old wetsuit, perhaps? Or, household door-and-window weather-strip foam tape with a peel-off backing. For glue, automotive weather-strip adhesive is the standard.

Finally, get an assortment of one of mankind's great inventions, the wire tie, with which you can pull things away from other things, thus restoring blessed silence.

Bad Smells

42. Cleanliness, water leaks, and mildew

The human nose is an exceedingly sensitive organ, so even the merest trace of an offensive odor can ruin your enjoyment of your car.

The first step in deodorizing is to remove everything from the interior that's not nailed down. Besides the floor mats, that means all the flotsam and jetsam under the seats, the fast-food wrappers from the console, and the odd dead mouse from the glove compartment. Then, do the same with the trunk.

Now, feel around for dampness. If an area of the carpet, or any other spot, is wet, a repair is called for. But that still doesn't relieve you of the task at hand, which is to get the inside of that car as clean as possible.

Vacuum thoroughly, of course. Just a few tiny fragments of food can cause olfactory distress. Then, you may want to consider renting (or even buying) one of those steam cleaners intended for household carpets and upholstery. As they say, "use as directed." A caveat on headliners: If yours is fabric and doesn't appear to be very well attached to the underside of the roof, you probably don't want to be pumping a bunch of hot vapor and detergent into that tenuous bond, then pulling it downward with a vacuum. You definitely don't want a sagging headliner.

That film on the inside of the glass? It definitely has an aroma, but is practically impervious to ordinary window cleaners. The only thing we've found that really cuts it is alcohol. Cover the dash and door panels with newspaper (alcohol can cause spots), then douse a clean cloth or pad of paper towels and get to work. Another benefit—you'll actually be able to see where you're going at night.

When you're done cleaning everything, leave the car parked out in the sun with the windows open for as long as possible.

Sure, life began in the sea, but in this situation water is always the enemy. It provides a habitat that'll grow all kinds of interesting botanical specimens. Think mold, mildew, and bacteria.

A common cause of carpet dampness, particularly on the passenger's side, is a clogged A/C condensate drain from the heater/evaporator box or tray. This may be from leaves and other vegetable detritus that finds its way into the ducts. We've seen it get so bad that you can hear sloshing while you're driving.

Sometimes the drain is simply a hole at the bottom of the box, or it may be a plastic hose or tube that sticks through a hole in the firewall. You've probably noticed a wet spot under the car that appears after you've parked on a hot day, and the drain will be directly above that. Use any kind of long probe (a knitting needle, one chopstick, a piece of a wire coat hanger) to clear it out.

Deteriorated or poorly fitting door, window, trunk lid, or hatch seals will allow H_2O infiltration. Have somebody hose down the car while you look around inside for drips. Also, look in the trunk or under trim panels for water getting in through the taillight assembly gaskets. Windshield leaks are another possibility, but resealing that big piece of glass is probably beyond what the average motorist will want to undertake, so you may want to visit a professional.

If your vehicle has a spare-tire well, it's a likely collection point for water. Remove the spare and check the condition of any rubber plugs in the bottom of the well. You can easily reseal them with RTV silicone caulk.

43. From the A/C?

Sometimes it's easy. You know exactly where the odor is coming from because you only get it through the A/C vents. Condensate moisture that promotes the growth of various microscopic organisms on the air conditioner's evaporator core is the problem. There are two ways to go here. You can buy deodorizers that you spray into the vents, but there's little chance that you'll deliver enough of a dose, where needed, to eradicate the flora. What professionals use are sprays that are injected directly into the heater box and really bathe that core. These are available at automotive parts jobbers or over the Internet, and can be quite expensive. They work well, though.

Another means of keeping the inside of the HVAC system

>> **Fungicide spray will eliminate A/C odors when applied to the evaporator core.**

dry is an "after-blower." It's an electronic module that you wire into the blower circuit that keeps the fan running for a predetermined time after you shut off the engine.

EXTRA: Bleach Bomb

Household bleach is the most potent weapon against whatever's growing in carpet or upholstery, but you can easily take out the dye with the odor. If the material is a light color, you might want to experiment with a highly diluted solution on an area that's hidden from view and see if you get whitening or spots. If not, sponge it into the suspect area, then use a wet/dry shop vacuum to extract it.

44. Smoke and filters

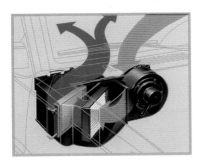

>> **Cabin air filter**

Smoking in a car with the windows closed is the equivalent of scientifically odorizing the interior. The smell permeates every fiber, including the vinyl itself and even those under vinyl, while redolent tar coats every surface. A thorough cleaning, as already described, is about all you can do—wait'll you see what you get off that glass!

Alas, as a used-car dealer we interviewed puts it, "If it's a heavy smoker, particularly cigars or a pipe, I don't think you can ever get the smell out." He's had a professional automotive deodorizing service treat the cars on his lot, but says he's only had about a 70 percent success rate with smells in general, less with smoke.

Many late models are equipped with cabin air filters. Changed yours lately? That job can be quite an exercise in automotive disassembly (check your owner's manual—you may have one and not know it), but there's a good chance the old filter has become odiferous.

Driving Tips

Take it Easy
45. Defensive driving

This amounts to a whole philosophy, a mind-set. Motorcyclists, who are obviously particularly vulnerable, often say that you should pretend that you're invisible. We don't think that takes it far enough. Instead, pretend that "they" (other motorists) are actively trying to kill you. Just figure the worst thing that other driver could do to jeopardize your safety, then proactively avoid it.

Defensive driving means leaving extra space between yourself and the car in front of you, giving pedestrians and bicyclists a wide berth even if it means stopping until the oncoming lane is clear, automatically taking your foot off the gas and getting ready to brake when you see somebody coming up to a stop sign too fast, and keeping watch as far ahead as you can see to give yourself more time to react in an emergency. In other words, it's anticipating what *might* happen.

This is a habit you can get yourself into. Think of it as the Zen of driving. You have to develop patience, let all that anger ("road rage") go. Abide by the old saying, "Live and let live." Not only will you avoid accidents, but the experience of driving, which is generally vastly underrated, will become less frustrating and much more enjoyable. Also, the smoothness of your actions that will naturally accompany the adoption of this philosophy will save gas and help your car last longer. The brake linings, for example, won't wear nearly as fast as they would if you were driving aggressively. There's no downside here.

Slippery Conditions
46. Skid physics

Although the increased stopping distances encountered in slippery conditions are very dangerous and require a defensive-driving turn of mind for safety, you should also beware of what was called, in the early days of motoring, "the dreaded side-slip." Once you get into a skid and find yourself traveling sideways and in no control whatsoever of your vehicle, all you can do is give yourself up to Lady Luck. Sure, many cars today come with stability control, but it can only do so much.

Let's avoid that situation. First, the basic rule: If you don't apply the brakes and don't try to turn, you can slow down by letting your foot off the gas, and your car will keep rolling in roughly the same direction as you've aimed it. It's when you try to force it to do something else that you test the traction available, and perhaps induce a hair-raising sideways ride.

Most importantly, you want to "scrape off" speed, which will be a whole lot easier if you're not going too fast in the beginning. Think about it this way: If you're doing 25 mph in the snow, it might take you a few minutes longer to reach your destination than if you're doing 45, but at the higher speed there's a good chance that you'll crash/hit somebody else/wrap yourself around a pole, and perhaps cause physical injury to yourself and others. This will take many days or weeks to correct, if it can be done at all. In other words, in bad conditions, it's idiotic not to slow down. If an impatient driver behind you wants to blow off his anger by tooting his horn, fine. Let him. Just don't speed up beyond what feels safe to you because another driver is harried and ill mannered. Hey, you're saving him or her from having an accident, too.

47. Installing tire chains

In the old days, it seemed that just about everybody kept tire chains in the trunk. With the improved traction of radial tires and front-wheel-drive cars, however, they've become a rarity. Still, tire chains will do an excellent job in bad conditions, particularly if ice is the problem—no matter how great the tread on the tires, rubber just can't bite in like steel. Municipalities sometimes close traffic to all passenger vehicles that don't have them.

You don't have to jack up the car to install chains, fortunately. Simply lay them down in the path of the driving wheels, then move the car forward until the tire is in the middle of the chains' length; bring the two ends together and attach them.

Saving Money

48. Calculating fuel mileage

Even if math wasn't your best subject, you can easily keep track of how many miles you are getting to the gallon (mpg). Keep a pen and pad handy in your car and simply record the number of miles you've covered since the last fill-up, and the number of gallons of gasoline or diesel fuel consumed in the process. For example, suppose you topped off the tank at 44,382 miles. Write down the miles (or, zero the trip odometer). When you fill up again, say at 44,605, record both the new mileage and the reading on the gas pump in gallons. Subtract the old mileage from the new mileage (if you've zeroed the odometer,

EXTRA: Eco Hobby

You can make a game, or even a hobby, out of conserving gasoline, which will reduce the tedium of long trips. Note the mpg you're getting, then apply the following driving patterns, check mpg again, and compare. If you're an average motorist who normally accelerates briskly and speeds down the highway unheedful of energy consumption, you can easily get another 5 or so mpg by just taking it easy. You'll reduce your chances of an accident, too.

just read it), then divide the number of miles traveled (223) by the number of gallons used (9.1) for the miles per gallon. In this case, 24.5 mpg.

49. Easy acceleration

You don't have to mash the accelerator to get up to cruising speed. It won't make any discernible difference in the length of time it takes to reach your destination. Applying the accelerator gradually and smoothly will save not only a considerable volume of fuel, but will also reduce the wear and tear on your vehicle. We've heard it said that you should pretend that there's a raw egg between your foot and the gas pedal.

50. Reduced cruising speed

Remember the "double nickel," as in 55 mph, the nationally mandated top speed during the fuel shortages of the 1970s? It saved millions of barrels of gasoline. We're not suggesting that you travel 55 where the limit is, say, 70, but reducing your cruising speed by just 5 mph will have a noticeable effect on fuel mileage without adding very much to your travel time. This is another calculation you can make.

EXTRA: Another Reason to Slow Down

Slowing down has another plus in that it both reduces your chance of having an accident, and, if you are so unfortunate as to crash anyway, your chance of being killed.

Accidents
51. Don't move

If there's no danger of fire (Do you smell gasoline? Is a puddle forming under the car?), and if you're not in the middle of speeding traffic where you might be rammed from behind, just stay put after an accident. This is especially important if you've been injured. Moving can cause broken bones to do internal damage, or make any internal injury worse.

Even in a case where you're not hurt, if you get out of your car in traffic, you could be hit by another car.

52. Fire

In the movies, practically every car crash ends in a huge fireball. Fortunately, that's decidedly not the case in the real world. It can and does happen, though, so you should have some notion of what to do if you find yourself in a burning car.

There's a misunderstanding about this situation that we feel compelled to try to fix. Some people just won't buckle up because they're afraid they'll be trapped in their seat belts if they're in an accident that involves fire. Actually, it's the unconscious people who burn. That is, those who didn't have their seat belts on and thus were knocked senseless upon impact.

So, what do you do if you are indeed conscious? First, unsnap your belt, which should be second nature. Then, decide which escape route exposes you to the least potential of being burned. That may mean scrambling over the seat and exiting at an opposite rear door. Even if your instant assessment of your injuries makes you think you've got a broken leg or back, if fire is about to engulf the car (or already has) MOVE! Once you hit the ground, run for it. If you've been licked by the flames, and perhaps your clothes are on fire, roll on the ground, preferably in the grass. If there's a pond, or even a puddle, nearby, jump in and roll.

53. Mayday!

Whether injuries are involved or not, you're still going to need help. Also, it's against the law to leave the scene of an accident until the police arrive, even if the car or cars are driveable. On the other hand, in all states, you are supposed to get the vehicles out of the roadway, if possible. If you have a working cell phone, immediately call 911 and give your location as clearly as you can.

Many states offer a more

direct alternative for traffic situations—not only accidents, but breakdowns, encounters with drunken or enraged drivers, etc. In Florida, for instance, you can dial *F-H-P (for Florida Highway Patrol, which translates into *3-4-7 on the keypad) and you'll be connected to the nearest FHP station. Other states will, obviously, use their own initials. If there's a serious injury involved, however, use 911.

54. Mum's the word

While it may be obvious to you who's at fault in an accident (if you've been rear-ended, it's always the other guy, no matter how stupid you might have been), there's simply no sense in blurting out either guilt or blame to the police, or to the other motorist. This may go to court, after all, and judging the subtleties of the legal system in the immediate aftermath of an accident is probably beyond your current mental state.

So, be polite and exchange information as required, but don't get into the subject of who's at fault. You'll thank us for this advice.

55. In the drink

The scariest motoring mishap we can think of besides a fire is ending up in the water. It happens a lot, and the number of fatalities would be reduced if everybody (a) wore seat belts so that they'd be conscious after the impact, and, (b) kept their wits about them.

If you've been knocked off a bridge, or have skidded into a

pond, you've got a little time to think because your car will contain a certain amount of air even though the weight of its running gear (engine and transmission) will pull it down—no car will float for long.

The traditional advice no longer applies. It held that: since you won't be able to open your door because of the pressure of the water against the outside, you should wind down your window and allow the car to fill while you take a few deep breaths of the remaining air bubble. Then, when there's water on both sides of the door, you should be able to open it, exit, and swim to the surface. Fine, except that most cars today have power windows, meaning electrically actuated, and nothing electrical is going to work once the car is submerged.

That's why they sell emergency tools that incorporate both a hammer to smash out a window, and a seat-belt slicer. Or, you could just keep a ball-peen hammer in the car. The trouble is, where do you store it? If you have it under the driver's seat, who knows where it might end up after the impact? It probably makes the most sense to keep it in the console, if you have one.

Keys, Doors, Hatches, and Windows

56. Can't turn the ignition key?

Ever since the ignition switch was incorporated into the steering column to thwart car thieves, being unable to turn the key has been a common complaint. What happens is that if you've parked with a front tire against the curb, or just in a certain way, the elasticity of the rubber will apply enough force to the locking mechanism to make it impossible to twist the key.

The answer is simple: Turn

>> If the key does not turn in the ignition switch, take the pressure off by twisting the steering wheel.

the steering wheel just a tiny bit away from the direction in which you feel a solid stop, then twist the key.

57. Hiding a spare key

This used to be easy. All you had to do was find a suitable spot under the car for mounting a magnetic key holder, or, since they tend to shake off so that they're not there when you need them, use a piece of copper wire as a twist tie to hold a spare key to the stabilizer bar, or any other convenient, yet not obvious, part of the chassis. Keys have always been made of noncorrosive metals, so exposure to the elements was never a problem.

Today, we have keys that contain electronic chips. (Those thieves causing complications again.) Not only are they expensive to duplicate, but they can't survive in the under-car environment nearly as well as a simple piece of chrome-plated brass. While a plain key duplicate may unlock the car, it won't start the engine.

You can bite the bullet as to the expense, but what about waterproof storage? You can wire a plain key duplicate under the car as above, which will get you inside the car, and keep a chip-equipped spare hidden somewhere in the interior.

58. Key fobs and remotes

These are nice, but remember that it wasn't that long ago that we didn't have them, and we got along fine. So, don't panic if nothing happens when you hit the unlock button. You can still get in by using the key the traditional way (we've heard rather amusing stories of people who made emergency phone calls for help in this situation—try not to become a laughingstock).

Of course, this is a desirable feature of your vehicle, and you want it to work. After three or four years, however, that key fob's battery is probably on the ragged edge of survival. It's a

>> **When your key fob quits, first try replacing the battery.**

simple matter to pop the key fob open (typically by inserting a dime in the seam between the two halves and prying or twisting it) and carefully remove the battery. Take it with you to any store that carries camera or watch batteries to make sure you get the right one.

59. Door-latch strikers

>> **A door rattle can often be eliminated by replacing the striker bolt.**

Most car doors latch onto striker bolts that are encircled with thin plastic or nylon wear tubes. When these materials disintegrate, which they always do, there'll be excessive clearance in the latching mechanism and a very good chance of a heavy rattle. For most vehicles, you can buy replacement striker bolts from the aftermarket (typically, you'll need a large Torx bit to remove them), but anything exotic will require a trip to the dealer.

EXTRA: Striker Reline

In a pinch, you can sometimes cut a short stub of PVC or CPVC plumbing pipe, split it, and force it over the existing bolt, but make sure the outside diameter is the same as that of the original part or you'll have problems getting the door to close.

60. Sagging hatch and hood supports

I nstead of the heavy, complicated system of springs and levers that were once used to hold up hoods and hatches against gravity, many cars now have light and simple pneumatic cylinders as supports. These work great at counterbalancing the weight of moveable body components—that is, until they don't. Over time, they'll gradually lose their compressed gas charge, with the result that the hatch or hood comes down with dangerous force.

Unless you drive some unusual vehicle, inexpensive replacements are available in

>> **Typically, you can remove pneumatic hood or hatch supports by prying out this clip.**

the aftermarket (in other words, at your local auto parts store), and performing the switch is easy. Simply hold the hatch up with a prop of a suitable length, pry the retaining clips off the old units, then install the new ones.

61. Power windows

You hit the button and get a hitching, grinding noise and the glass just sort of trembles, or there's no sound whatsoever. Regardless, that window isn't going up. Typical power window failures are: drag, a breakdown in the mechanism, or no electrical activity.

The most obvious and lowest-tech problems involve weather-stripping gaskets and channels. These take a beating. Besides continuous mechanical abuse, there's the general environment—heat, UV, ice, dirt. So, after a while, they tear, crack, split, come unglued, and buckle, typically bunching up, jamming the tracks and effectively stopping the glass from running up and down. This may lead to blown fuses or a damaged mechanism.

If you're lucky, you might be able to fix this kind of thing without getting inside the door. Perhaps you've noticed that the window channel liner has moved down from the top of the door, leaving a gap (this will cause an annoying wind whistle). Grasp the liner with pliers, pull it back up (you might have to try to raise the window at the same time), and glue it in place with contact cement.

In cases where the motor's power is marginal, it's possible that just spraying silicone lube in the channel liners will get things moving again.

If you're not so lucky, it's time to go in, as surgeons say. That means removing the inner door panel, a job most motorists won't want to tackle.

In cases where you hear nothing when you press any of the switches, the logical first step is to check the fuse for the power window circuit. If it's blown, you could just replace it and hope for

EXTRA: Swapping Switches

>> **In some cases, power window switch parts can swap to the driver's door.**

On some common models, the driver's-side window switch rocker tends to break. After all, it gets by far the most use. The carmakers will say you have to replace the whole driver's switch panel, but that can cost as much as a set of cheap tires. You can often remove the panel, take out a rocker that operates one of the rear windows, and snap it in where it's needed— nobody ever sits back there but your mother-in-law anyway, right? And she can still control her own window.

the best, but you haven't ascertained the reason for the overload. The channel problem mentioned above, perhaps?

A related possibility is the circuit breaker in the motor. It may trip under undue stress, and it can take a couple of minutes to reset. Once again, look for conditions that increase drag.

Check the switches themselves if some windows respond and others don't. If you've ever had occasion to take one apart, you've seen that they appear to be quite flimsy considering the importance of their job, their frequency of use, and the amount of current they're asked to control.

62. Power locks

Central locking systems are so common we forget how inconvenient it was to either stretch across the seats and push those buttons down, or to actually walk around the car and lock all the doors.

Most systems are purely electrical, using a solenoid (an electromagnetic device that converts voltage into physical movement) to pull the locking lever to the locked position, although a few makes, such as Mercedes-Benz, perform this function by means of a pneumatic unit.

If nothing happens when you try to lock the car from the driver's door, see if it works from any of the other doors. Yes? Then the problem is in the driver's door switch. In cases where you get no action anywhere, check the appropriate fuse. If just one door quits locking, the trouble is probably the solenoid itself.

EXTRA: Clean the Contacts

Some vehicles, such as full-size vans, use button-type contacts to make an electrical connection between the doors and the chassis wiring. These can typically corrode to the point that continuity is broken. The repair is as simple as cleaning the contacts with sandpaper (you can even scrape them with a key in a pinch).

See and Be Seen
63. Wipers

Poor wiper action is extremely annoying, not to mention dangerous. Where blade replacement is concerned, there's an important point: If the rubber ever tears off completely, say, from snow and ice, any metal parts of the wiper that may happen to contact the glass are going to wear an unsightly groove in the windshield that can never, ever, be removed. So you can think of this as preventative maintenance. In urban areas with nasty acid and ozone in the air, or in the sunny South, this should be done quite frequently (perhaps on an annual basis) because those environmental conditions cause the rubber to oxidize and dry out.

The first thing to do is measure the old blades so you can get the right replacements. Check both sides because in some cars they're of different lengths. Now, you have some cost/value choices to make. In many cases, you can just buy

>> Measure your old blades before shopping for new ones.

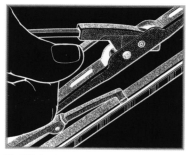

>> **With the shepherd's-crook type, depress a tab to release the blade.**

refills for your original blade assemblies. This will be the cheapest route. On the other hand, you may have trouble getting the exact replacement refill, and installation can be tricky. As a result, most people today are opting for whole blade assemblies. The other choice is whether to go regular or premium. The price difference can be substantial, so compare the expected life and warranty information.

Getting the old wiper assemblies off and the new ones on properly isn't so easy unless you know the trick. On the pin-mount type, you can usually just use a key to press in against the little coil spring found at the midpoint hinge, which will release the blade. On the shepherd's-crook type, you depress a tab and move the

EXTRA: Wiper Tension

In some cases, the installation of new wiper assemblies results in poor squeegee action. The problem? The new assemblies hold the blade arch more stiffly than the old, and the fatigued and rusted hold-down springs in the arms can't deal with the pressure. Believe it or not, there's such a thing as a wiper-arm pressure tester, and fresh springs are available.

blade downward on the arm until it's free.

A noisy wiper motor (usually mounted high on the firewall) can make you not want to drive the car, yet in most cases replacement is a pretty simple job.

64. Windshield washers

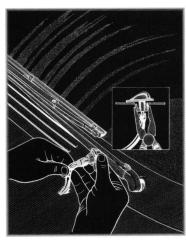

>> **All it takes is common sense to repair a windshield washer hose or nozzle.**

A washer that won't might just be clogged, either in the nozzles or lines, or at the pump pickup. Those lines are probably brittle enough to leak at their connections by now, too.

If the washer pump itself is bad, you'll naturally think about replacing it with an OE (Original Equipment—in other words, from the car dealer's parts department) unit first. One problem: The price may be high enough to make you decide to just carry a bottle of Windex™ with you. Aftermarket universals are the solution. They're inexpensive and easy to install.

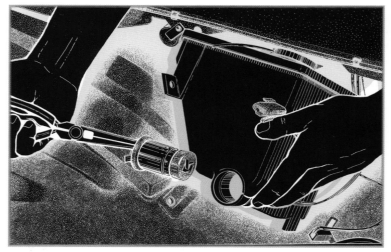

>> **When your windshield washer pump gives out, shop for an aftermarket universal unit, which will be less expensive than buying an original-equipment pump.**

65. That tenacious windshield haze

That film on the inside of the glass is practically impervious to ordinary window cleaners, and even the special automotive aerosols we've tried can't seem to get it off. The only thing we've found that really cuts it is regular rubbing alcohol. Cover the dash and door panels with newspaper (alcohol can cause spots), open all windows, then douse a clean cloth or pad of paper towels and get to work.

66. Windshield bull's-eyes

Years ago, if you were unlucky enough to have a stone fly up and cause a round bull's-eye in your windshield, the only possible remedy was a whole new piece of glass, which was an expensive proposition even back then.

So, the invention of epoxy and acrylic windshield repairs was a boon to the common man. In many cases, it's actually possible to fix that bull's-eye, star, flower, or BB chip by injecting a clear adhesive filler right into it. Not only does this

>> **Follow kit instructions to the letter.**

keep the damage from getting worse, perhaps from water infiltration, but it often results in a practically invisible repair.

Numerous kits are available that allow you to do this job yourself, and they all come with detailed instructions, which you must follow to the letter. Since you'll be saving so much money over what a new windshield would cost, we recommend that you spring for the best kit you can find.

67. Reattaching the rearview mirror

Have you ever come out to your car, typically on a hot, sunny day, only to find that your rearview mirror has fallen off the windshield? Sure, you can drive without it, but not safely.

Reattachment is fairly easy. Go to an auto parts store, or perhaps the automotive department of a mass merchandiser, and buy a kit especially made for the job. It'll contain vials of super adhesive and primer/accelerant to speed the cure. Might as well read the instructions, which, along with the following, should make everything go smoothly.

Most mirrors dovetail to the baseplate and are retained with an Allen screw (make sure you have the right size Allen wrench). Before you loosen the screw and slide the baseplate out of the mirror assembly, note the plate's original position—rounded side up, for example. Make sure you also keep track of which side of the plate goes against the glass.

Before you proceed, look for evidence of the original adhesive to give you the proper mounting

>> **Mask or mark the original position of the rearview mirror baseplate. Typically, the mirror assembly is retained by an Allen screw.**

point. On the outside of the windshield, outline the spot with either a grease pencil or strips of masking tape. Now, clean off the old adhesive using a single-edge razor blade and isopropyl alcohol. Do the same with the back of the mounting plate.

Cover the dash with newspaper. Bend the tube that contains the primer/accelerant to break the vial, then apply to the baseplate and the windshield using the applicator tube's tip. Allow it to dry for 5 minutes. Next, coat the back of the baseplate with a generous layer of the adhesive, press it firmly against the windshield, and hold it for at least 2 minutes. Don't worry if some of the glue squishes out because you can trim it later with your razor blade. Let the bond cure for as long as possible, especially if the weather's cold. Overnight would be good. Finally, slide the mirror over the baseplate and tighten the screw.

>> **A primer/accelerant ensures the bond. Make sure you attach the correct side of the baseplate to the windshield.**

Headlights

In states with vehicle inspection programs, you'll be tipped off to improper headlight aiming. If you should happen to be doing this yourself, take a walk around the car. Look for anything that affects proper ride height: low tires, sagging springs, or several overweight relatives in the back seat. Headlights don't go out of alignment by themselves, so faulty aiming is an indication of some unusual condition.

Many late models will warn you if a headlight is out. Otherwise, it makes sense to drive up to a wall once in a while with the lights on to be sure you see a bright spot on each side, high and low beam. If, unbeknownst to you, you've been driving with a dead headlight, replacing it can make you feel like you've just had cataracts removed.

68. Sealed beam

For many decades, sealed beam was the headlight standard mandated by the U.S. Department of Transportation, the only changes being the "quad" headlights that first appeared in 1958, and the adoption of rectangular bulbs and quartz halogens in the 1970s.

Replacement would be simple if it weren't for rusty, seized screws. So, before you begin to remove the grille trim and the frame that holds the defunct bulb in place, spray the fasteners with penetrating oil. It can also be difficult to pull the connector off the lugs on the back of the bulb, so you may need to pry with a screwdriver. It wouldn't hurt to wear your safety glasses.

>> The sealed beam headlight served us well for decades.

>> Once the trim is off, replacing a sealed beam isn't difficult.

69. Composite

This big improvement in safety and service is on most late models. It consists of a small, easily replaceable quartz-halogen bulb inside a plastic housing that typically incorporates a stylish reflector and lens. The bulb's socket is mounted in a plastic holder that locks into the headlight assembly with a twist of the wrist.

>> Replacement of composite bulbs can be done with a twist of the wrist. Make sure you don't touch the new bulb with your bare fingers.

117

EXTRA: Avoid Fingerprints

When it comes to replacing a composite headlamp, the important thing to remember is to strenuously avoid touching the new bulb with your fingers. It seems that the oil from your skin will carbonize and cause hot spots on the surface of the glass, which will soon result in a crack and a blown bulb. So, leave the protective sleeve on the new bulb until it's installed, and perhaps even wear clean gloves for the procedure.

70. High-intensity discharge

Found mostly on upscale vehicles, this supremely bright and sharply focused type of headlight gives off a bluish light. Unlike conventional headlamps, there's no filament to burn out. Instead, the light is generated by incandescent gases in a quartz tube—almost 20,000 volts are required to get the plasma started!

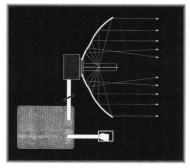

>> **Superbright and accurately focused high-intensity-discharge headlights should last the life of the car.**

Aside from mechanical damage due to a collision, there should be no need to do anything whatsoever with this type of headlight. If you should have occasion to remove one for any purpose, however, make absolutely sure the switch is off, the battery is disconnected, and the ballast connectors are unplugged, or you're risking a dangerous, high-voltage shock.

71. Signal lights

It's a good idea to do a once-a-month walk-around inspection of your vehicle to make sure all the lights are working. Check the directionals on both sides. (If one bulb has burned out, you may get very rapid blinking when signaling for that side.) If you suspect a brake light, back up close to a wall at night and watch in your mirrors as you hit the brake pedal repeatedly.

Replacing these bulbs may

>> **In some cases, you'll have to remove the lens to get at the bulb.**

>> **More bulbs are becoming accessible from the inside.**

119

involve taking out the external screws that secure the lens, or simply twisting a plastic socket inside the car and pulling it out for access. To extract the bulb, usually you press down on it, turn it counterclockwise, and pull it out. Wear a glove, or use a piece of a bicycle inner tube to grasp the bulb to keep you from getting cut if that fragile glass should break. If you haven't looked up the proper bulb type in your owner's manual, you can read it off the base of the old one.

EXTRA: Bad Connection

Corroded sockets can sometimes prevent a lamp from lighting. You can scrape the rust out with a knife, or use sandpaper wrapped around the end of your finger.

Maintenance Matters

They Last and Last

72. The truth about durability

Believe it or not, you can pretty well figure that with proper maintenance any modern automotive engine will go a couple of hundred thousand miles without a major internal repair, such as a valve, ring, or bearing job. At 15,000 miles per year—fairly heavy usage— that's 13 years and four months; or, at 10,000 per year, two solid decades.

How can that be? you cry. What about planned obsolescence? Well, if you can get over the sentiments you've probably heard since you were old enough to pay attention, the truth is simply that the car manufacturers want to make the best, most trouble-free and durable products possible—

within reasonable limits of costs and profitability. It just happens to be a fact that if a make gets a reputation as a soon-to-be heap that begins to fall apart as you drive it home from the dealer, nobody will buy another one. Auto executives know that, and live in fear of the bad reputation phenomenon.

But, in the past, that wasn't enough to get the average vehicular lifespan up to much more than 100,000 miles. The technology, chemistry, and materials just weren't there. Now, not only do we have vastly superior motor oil and filtration, we also have an air/fuel mixture so precisely controlled that the oil is never diluted with gasoline, nor is the film of lubricant washed off the cylinder walls by the presence of excessive fuel.

In past decades, however, even if you were able to coax an engine over the 100,000-mile hump, by that time, chances are the body would have rusted away to the point of serious safety compromises. Again, things have changed. New sheet-metal treatments, high-tech finishes, advanced chemical sealers and caulks, better body drains, more use of plastics, and so on all keep Mother Nature at bay for far longer than was the case in the old days.

Other things hold up incredibly well now, too. Modern spark plugs, low-friction steering and suspension joints, serpentine accessory belts, and exhaust system components, to name a few, go many more miles and years than did those of older models. One glaring exception

is brakes, which still require at least as much regular service as they did in the past. With some Euro sport models and heavy SUVs, you might need to have the brake linings (the parts of your brake system that wear, called "pads" with disc brakes, and "shoes" with drums) and maybe the discs themselves replaced on an almost annual basis. Follow our advice in the "Driving Tips" section (pg. 91) to reduce this tendency.

But many of these admirable advances in design and materials can be scuttled by poor maintenance. Neglecting oil changes, or allowing the cooling system to deteriorate to the point of overheating are two of the most damaging things you can do—they can blow all that vast durability potential away, and leave you facing a repair bill that you won't believe possible. As some professionals put it, "Fluids are cheap, parts and labor are expensive." In many cases, hideously so.

We know you've heard this before, perhaps from an older male relative, but that doesn't make it any less true: Regular maintenance will save you far more than it costs. With engines and transmissions/transaxles especially, this can easily amount to many thousands of dollars.

So, have the engine oil, transmission fluid, coolant, and brake fluid changed at least as often as your owner's manual recommends. We say "at least" because some carmakers have pushed the limits to be able to advertise low maintenance costs. For example, you might see a recommended transmission-fluid change interval of 100,000 miles. That's gambling with some pretty big money.

Engine and Transmission

73. Oil changes

S ome years ago, the auto companies were making points with consumers by showing low annual operating costs. To further this effort, the mileage between oil changes was pushed up and up in owner's manuals, all the way to an asking-for-trouble 10,000 and more miles in some cases.

There was some hedging, however. The long intervals were for "normal" driving. (We don't know anybody that normal.) But a different, much shorter schedule was offered for severe service (frequent idling, stop and go, trips of 10 miles or less, sustained high speeds in hot weather, trailer towing—in other words, the way most people operate their vehicles), typically every 3,000 miles or three months. That was more like it from a real-world standpoint.

Even the most highly evolved engine on the road still has to start cold, then gets hot, still makes blow-by and huge quantities of water vapor, still has small passages that lube must go through, still breathes dirty air, still . . . you get the picture. Therefore, we don't like to suggest that you go much over 5,000 miles between changes.

Modern motor oils are a lot more than a boiled-down dinosaur. They contain a blend of fortifying additive that include detergent dispersants to pick up dirt and keep it from collecting in lumps, viscosity

improvers to reduce the rate of thickness change from one temperature to another, extreme pressure agents to increase film strength and keep the oil from being squeezed out of load-bearing joints, pour-point depressants to make the lube more enthusiastic about flowing out of a can or into a bearing at low temperatures, defoamants to control frothing, antioxidants to help prevent overheated and churned-up oil from thickening and forming tar and varnish, and friction modifiers to cut internal drag.

Since 1970, the American Petroleum Institute (API) has used basically the same oil

>> **Oil container API label**

125

EXTRA: Light Oil

There's been a switch to the 5W-30, or 0W-20 viscosity recommendation from various carmakers over the last decade or so, the benefits being better mpg and reduced start-up wear. Here's the story: Most wear occurs when you first turn the key, no matter how hot or cold the weather, and this lighter grade will definitely get into those moving parts faster. At minus 15°F, for instance, 5W-30 takes 10 seconds to reach the rocker arms, compared to 20 seconds with 10W-30. But the interesting thing is that 5W-30 is flowing freely to the rockers in 40 seconds, whereas with 10W-30 it takes 3 minutes! And it provides the same high-temperature protection as 10W-30.

classification system we have today. Under the "S" (Service) heading, grades range from SA (pretty useless) to SL (the best at the time of this writing). Viscosity is classified by the Society of Automotive Engineers (SAE). There are two ratings, one for winter (SAE 0W, 5W, 10W, and 20W), and another for the rest of the seasons (SAE 20, 30, 40, and 50). Multiviscosity oils have what's known as a high viscosity index, which means their fluidity and body change little from one temperature extreme to the other.

The space at the bottom of the API "donut" symbol on the container is reserved for an oil's fuel-saving rating. If it just says "Energy Conserving," it cuts friction enough to increase mpg 1.5 percent over a standard test-reference oil. But the next level is "Energy Conserving II," which can mean up to a 3 percent improvement.

In spite of having been around for half a century, the market penetration of synthetic oil is still very low. That's because it costs at least twice as much per quart as you're used to paying, so companies that want to sell it have to prove that it's a whole lot better.

But in most ways, synthetic oil *is* a lot better. Chemists "build" PAO (polyalphaolefin) and ester-base stocks with properties that are predictable and stable. Oil thickens with use because its lighter, more volatile fractions boil off, but some synthetic formulations exhibit only one tenth the thickening of conventional oil. This low volatility can also cut consumption, because most of the lube an engine in good condition uses is lost as it flashes into vapor at the piston rings.

Cold-weather performance is also impressive. At minus 50°F, a good synthetic is still fluid, whereas regular oil has the consistency of peanut butter. Synthetic blends are a less-expensive compromise.

74. Coolant changes

A neglected cooling system can cause problems that range from insufficient heater output and a fouled coolant temperature sensor (which can throw the engine management system off) to a blown head gasket, scored cylinders, and a cracked block, so it's foolish economy to put off maintenance.

If that coolant looks bad (it's supposed to be a nice, bright

EXTRA: A Dollar Well Spent

>> Use distilled or deionized water to mix with antifreeze.

There's no sense buying that nice, fresh antifreeze, then mixing it with tap water (fifty-fifty is the proper ratio no matter where you live), which typically contains chlorine, fluoride, and lots of dissolved minerals. Spend a dollar and buy a gallon of distilled or deionized water at the grocery store.

color, not brown and rusty), chances are it's been in there longer than the two years most manufacturers have been recommending for decades. With all the aluminum and the increased heat loads found in modern cars, it looked for a while like annual coolant changes were going to be the only way to head off problems. But just the opposite has happened: Antifreeze has become so sophisticated that the intervals are being extended in many cases. For example, GM's Long-Life spec, based on Organic Acid Technology (OAT) (it's orange, not the green/gold you might be used to), ranges from 100,000 to 150,000 miles!

The term "antifreeze" itself is an unfortunate misnomer because it does a lot more than just keep the icebergs away. It curtails corrosion, lubes the water-pump seal, and raises the boiling point. So, even if you live in a tropical climate, a fifty-fifty mixture is still necessary.

75. Today's tune-up

Strictly speaking, there's no such thing as a tune-up on cars built since the early 1980s. The term suggests adjustments in spark timing, fuel mixture, and idle speed, none of which is possible anymore. But the job seems to have sacred-cow status. It seems to be embedded in human consciousness, and it just won't die. We're sure people will be walking into shops for many years to come asking for a tune-up, just as they've heard their parents do.

So, a tune-up has morphed into a bundle of maintenance services, which is not a bad thing. What you'll get is new spark plugs, a valve-lash adjustment on cars that require it and perhaps a thorough cleaning of the throttle body (deposits here can interfere with idle quality), and an intake-tract cleaning treatment. All the important fluids will be checked and perhaps changed, also.

The thing to remember about a tune-up is that if it fixes a problem, fine. But it isn't intended as a repair. It's maintenance.

76. The truth about spark plugs

Most manufacturers brag that their late models can go 100,000 miles on the original spark plugs. True, the plugs may indeed last that long. But what about the threads they screw into? If even one plug is seized, you may be in for a multi–thousand dollar job as it's likely that the cylinder head will have to be removed for thread repair. It might be possible to find a shop that'll be willing to try to do a thread repair with the cylinder head in

›› If you change your own spark plugs, put a dab of antiseize compound on the threads.

place, thus saving you many hundreds of dollars, but you'll have to ask around for somebody who knows what he or she is doing.

EXTRA: A Realistic Interval

Many professionals are now saying it makes more sense to install new plugs every 60,000 miles to help avoid the financial catastrophe of thread repair.

77. Timing-belt replacement

A snapped timing belt (a toothed, fiberglass-reinforced rubber belt that drives the overhead camshafts of many engines) will often cause extremely expensive damage, plus you'll be broken down on the road. Traditionally, timing-belt replacement was recommended every 60,000 miles, but late models are often okay for 100,000 or so. Take the time to read the maintenance section

>> **Change the timing belt at the recommended interval to prevent very expensive internal engine damage.**

in your owner's manual, and you may save enough for a nice vacation.

78. Transmission fluid changes

This is another maintenance item that can spare you a monumental repair bill. Late-model drivetrains run at much higher temperatures than did their predecessors, and it's generally accepted that 90 percent of transmission failures are due to overheating. The oxidation rate (which determines the useful lubrication life) of

EXTRA: Fresh Gear Lube

Some manufacturers recommend that the gear lubricant in manual transmissions and transaxles be changed every 24,000 miles, while others say you never need to touch it. But, really, how different is one make from another? Not enough to make this a bad idea for every car. Again, think about going synthetic.

automatic transmission fluid (ATF) doubles for every 20°F increase over the normal operating temperature of 175°F, which means fluid that's formulated to last 100,000 miles will only go 50,000 at 195°F, or 3,000 at 275°F.

Add the astronomical jump in transmission repair costs over the last couple of decades (blame the proliferation of front-wheel-drive transaxles and complicated overdrive units) and you can see that you might avoid the biggest repair bill

you've ever seen by doing more frequent ATF and filter changes, and maybe even installing an aftermarket cooler.

Some automakers say ATF changes only need to be done at 100,000 miles unless the vehicle is subjected to severe service (trailer towing, stop-and-go driving), in which case 30,000 is the recommended interval. Our opinion? This should be done every 30,000 miles, period. Also, consider spending the extra money to upgrade to synthetic ATF.

Tires
79. Inflation

While we have to suggest that you follow the recommended inflation pressures listed in your owner's manual and on the driver's-side door or door pillar, we can mention that many professional service shops simply put 35 psi (pounds per square inch) all around in every car, regardless.

The important thing here is to neither neglect, nor overdo. If inflation pressure is too low, your tires will wear out prematurely, steering and handling will be less accurate and safe than they should be, you'll burn more gas, and the car just won't be fun to drive. On the other hand, if you overinflate you're going to get excessive tread wear in the center of the tire, poor traction, and a hard ride.

80. Rotation

Here's something that can save you considerable money and isn't expensive or complicated. It's in the nature of vehicular dynamics that a tire in one position on the car will wear at a different rate than those at the other positions. Rotating the tires will distribute the wear more evenly and allow you to get maximum mileage out of the tread.

Some rotation patterns include the spare, while others do not. Once again, consult your owner's manual.

81. Buying tires

With so many brands, so many outlets, and so many ads everywhere, buying tires can be bewildering. You might as well start by collecting ads. Read the fine print. Does that low advertised price include balancing and new valve stems? How about free rotation for some period of time?

Next, if your regular service provider sells tires, ask his advice. Some shops only do tires as a convenience for their customers, so they don't have the volume to offer a big discount. If the difference isn't too large, however, you should think seriously about keeping all your automotive business with your provider. Loyal customers are naturally treated the best, now and forever.

Otherwise, call the various tire dealers and mass merchandisers. Have the size handy (copy it off the sidewall) and ask if there are any special deals available. Most we've talked to will give you a quote over the phone.

Where prices are concerned, make sure you're comparing apples to apples. Every regular passenger car tire (except snow tires) is rated for tread life, traction, and temperature resistance under Uniform Tire Quality Grade (UTQG) standards established by the U.S. Department of Transportation (USDOT) and National Highway Traffic Safety Administration (NHTSA). "Tread life" means just what it says, and the higher the number the better. "Traction" refers to the tire's grip when stopping in a straight line on a wet surface, and has nothing to do with performance in curves, or "dig" on hard acceleration. This rating ranges from AA, the highest, down to C. The temperature resistance rating represents how well the tire deals with high heat (not just ambient temperature, but also that created by underinflation or heavy loads) and high speeds. Any tire sold in the U.S. must at least meet the C rating, meaning it shouldn't disintegrate until between 85 and 100 mph. If you need to go faster than that on public roads, we don't approve, but at least opt for B (100 to 115 mph), or A (over 115 mph).

The flashy wheel and tire mania is seemingly everywhere. If you're ever tempted to join the club, think twice. It's not just the incredible expense we're talking about, it's that those fancy rims and rubber-band tires will affect the carefully engineered dynamics of your vehicle. The most important factor here is the rolling diameter of the tires. Not only will a change from stock throw your speedometer off, it can play havoc with your Antilock Brake System (ABS) and any stability control system you might have. Other potential problems are the offset of the new rim (Does it stick out farther from the axle flange?), and the lack of pneumatic "give" in high-performance tires—the wheel makes up much more of the diameter of the assembly, and it's solid, not flexible.

EXTRA: Pulsation and Twisted Discs

If, a short time after leaving the shop where you bought your new tires, you notice that you've got a pulsation in the brake pedal that wasn't there before, somebody probably cranked up his monster air-impact wrench and way overtightened your lug nuts, probably in the wrong pattern, too, which has twisted your brake discs. Complain. Better yet, head off the possibility by offering the tire tech a tip if he'll torque (that is, tighten with a calibrated wrench) the lugs by hand, and in the proper crisscross pattern.

82. Brake fluid changes

As you know unless you're not following automotive progress, just about all newer vehicles have ABS (Antilock Braking Systems). Fortunately, the electronics involved have shown themselves to be pretty dependable, except for damaged wheel-speed sensors. Most of the problems are hydraulic—water, corrosion, and deposits in the control unit.

That makes brake fluid changes a hot topic. Where once the domestic manufacturers made nary a mention of the need to dump the old stuff periodically (or even during a brake job), now they're giving intervals, something the imports

EXTRA: Turkey Baster

If you're not persuaded as to the cost/benefit justification for brake fluid flushing, at least get yourself a turkey baster at the dollar store and take a few minutes to remove the old fluid from the master cylinder's reservoir, then refill it with fresh. Since the fluid moves around inside the system, this will help reduce the moisture content. Don't drip any on the paint!

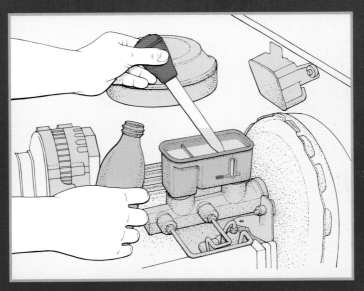

>> **ABS is a safety breakthrough, but the control unit is very expensive to replace.**

>> **Having your brake hydraulic system flushed periodically helps insure against a costly ABS repair.**

have been doing for decades. It's the only way to get rid of moisture, rust, and the ashy residue of burned glycol.

This has always been sensible maintenance, but now the presence of ABS is a further justification. Fluid changes are cheap insurance against extremely expensive repairs.

Recommended intervals range from one to three years.

Body

83. Washing and waxing

Did you ever notice that your car seems to run better after you've washed it? That's probably because the improved aesthetics enhance your whole automotive experience.

But washing a car shouldn't

be a mindless expending of elbow grease. There are actually a few rules to follow:

- Don't do it in the sun or you'll get streaks the likes of which you've never seen before.

- Don't use a brush with abrasive plastic bristles or you'll damage the base-coat/clearcoat finish. It will be fine for your wheels and tires, however.

- If the car is not too dirty, use plain water and a sponge. If that's not potent enough, use mild soap, not strong detergents (such as for clothing).

- A truly filthy car should be washed from the bottom up to avoid streaks.

- Use a chamois or a regular towel to dry off the water, which will keep spots from forming.

Back in the days of enamel and lacquer paint jobs, you could really feel satisfied with

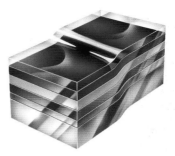

>> **The base-coat/clearcoat finishes of modern cars do not need the traditional methods of paint maintenance.**

waxing your car. You'd probably have been using wax that contained a mild abrasive compound that polished off the oxidized finish, leaving what amounted to fresh paint.

Now, with base-coat/clearcoat finishes, that tradition has got to change. The last thing you want to do is abrade off that transparent top coat, which is probably only a couple of mils thick. Many people have simply given up polishing their cars altogether, and just wash them. Those of you who take pride in your vehicle's

EXTRA: Nix Abrasive Brushes

A note on car washes: Don't go to a car wash that uses automated plastic brushes as they'll abrade the clearcoat off. If you go to one regularly, you might end up with a finish that looks worse than that of a car that never gets washed at all.

appearance, however, can still shine it up without doing damage. Throw away those old cans and bottles of cleaner waxes that have been in your garage practically forever, and buy some new products intended for clearcoat finishes. Read the label carefully. You may want to get plain wax, such as carnuba, or a cleaner wax that contains a chemical intended to remove oxidation.

You don't wax a dirty car, so wash and dry it thoroughly. We know this is a pleasant outdoor activity, but if you don't have a shady spot available, you'll have to do it in the garage, because applying wax to a hot finish out

in the sun will turn into a disaster.

Start with the roof. Don't do an area so big at one time that you can't buff off the haze within a few minutes. If the wax didn't come with an applicator, you can use a damp kitchen sponge. You don't have to rub as much or as hard as your ancestors did with old-fashioned enamel and lacquer because you're not trying to get down to fresh paint. What you're doing, instead, is filling in the minute scratches in the surface of the clearcoat with polymers. So, you're just applying the wax or polish. Be careful not to get any wax on rubber, textured plastic, or flat black areas.

When the wax dries to a haze, buff it with a soft cloth or towel. Don't stop for lunch in between, or that whitish residue will become very difficult to get off. An old toothbrush applied around nameplates and trim adds the finishing touch.

84. Paint chips

Don't let these exposed areas where the finish has chipped off go so long that they develop into a real problem. With modern base-coat/clearcoat finishes, there's a right way and an easy way to take care of dings. The right way requires a great deal of time, patience, and skill, so it isn't appropriate for anyone but the enthusiast. The easy way is, well, easy. While it won't result in a perfectly invisible repair, it will sure help improve the appearance of the car and it will keep rust from taking over.

The first step is to buy a bottle of paint that matches your car exactly, which may require a trip to the dealership. If the chip is down to bare metal, use a tiny piece of very fine emery paper (400-grit, or up) to roughen the surface and sand off any rust, but stay inside the chip. Use some household isopropyl ("rubbing") alcohol and a paper

>> **If the damage is small, try to fix it with a bottle of touchup paint instead of the big project of spray painting.**

141

towel to clean the area. Thoroughly shake the bottle of touchup paint, then apply it carefully. Don't put it on so thick that it sags or runs. You may need to do multiple coats, but wait a day in between applications.

85. Rust spots

Ouch! Rust is the enemy of steel, as if Mother Nature wants to take back her iron ore. It may not look too bad at first, but, like cancer in an organism, it'll inevitably spread until it becomes serious. To continue the analogy, you'll have to use both surgery and chemotherapy to stop the hungry advance of that oxidation.

The first thing to do if rust appears at the bottom of a door panel, rocker panel, or any other hollow section, is to get some light and air in there. In other words, dry it out. Dirt, leaves, rust flakes and even road salt inside sheet-metal panels form what's called a "poultice" that holds moisture and continues to promote corrosion even in dry weather. You won't have any lasting luck with a repair if you don't remove this accumulation, which may require some interior disassembly, or, if it's gone far enough, the reaming out of the hole from the outside. Of course, you're in for some amateur bodywork in that case, typically involving Bondo® or an equivalent polyester filler, but that's beyond the scope of this book.

Further, nothing you do will last if you don't get rid of, or neutralize, every trace of iron oxide. You can sand until the surface is clear, but we recommend that you also apply a rust-converting chemical, the most common being Ospho™

142

and Naval Jelly™. There are other products that do basically the same thing, but also leave a rust-resistant coating. Read the labels of whatever's available at your local auto store, or in the automotive section of a mass merchandiser.

>> **A rust converter prevents corrosion from spreading, but needs to be painted after it dries.**

While you're there, decide what you need in the way of paint. If the spot is the size of a dime or smaller, you'll do best with a bottle of touchup (there'll be a suitable brush in the cap). Bigger? Then buy spray cans of automotive primer and touchup paint. In either case, make sure you get the exact match for your year and make, or you'll regret it. If an exact match is not available in those stores, visit the new car dealer's parts department and order it.

With a brush, follow the advice in #84, pg 141, "Paint chips." If you're spraying, do so on a nice day and well out of the wind. Use a light touch on the spray nozzle, and sweep the can swiftly across the area, keeping it about 10 inches away from the surface. Starting with the primer, make a couple of passes, then let that coat dry. Otherwise, you'll get drips. Ditto for the finish paint.

86. Drain holes

If you were designing an automobile from scratch, you might consider trying to make every part of the body absolutely waterproof. That wouldn't be realistic, however, because of the need for windows and a hood and trunk lid that can be opened. So, you'd have to adopt the "water in, water out" philosophy. That is, you'd incorporate water drains into the bottom of hollow panels and elsewhere.

Great . . . until they become clogged with leaves and other detritus. Then, a poultice forms

>> **Make sure drain holes in doors and body panels are clear to prevent internal rust.**

that holds moisture and makes corrosion inevitable. So, every time you wash your car, stick a toothpick, a stiff wire, or any other kind of probe up into the drains to make sure they're open.

87. Dealing with professionals

With cars so complex today, most motorists, and especially those at the lower end of the

mechanical-inclination scale, are going to be compelled to enlist the aid of professional technicians from time to time.

So, you should have some idea of how the business of auto repair is run, and how to communicate with your tech, shop owner, or service writer.

Flat rates

The length of time a job should take, and therefore the labor charge, is established by what's called the flat rate system. When a shop owner, service writer, or technician estimates a job, he or she will look it up in a flat rate manual (usually on DVD or online, these days), multiply the number of hours by the shop's hourly charge, and add parts and supplies costs. While publishers generally don't make this information available to consumers, it's not exactly confidential, either. The trouble is, you'd have to pay a substantial amount to buy the books or disks, and you might only use them a few times in a car's life.

Choosing a shop

Just like doctors and lawyers, some shop owners and technicians are good, some not so good. Ask your friends and neighbors who gives them the most satisfactory automotive service. Visit any shop you're considering and see if you're treated politely and feel comfortable there. If not, you won't want to be there when you've got a problem.

Establishing a mutually beneficial relationship

As with most things in life, communication is crucial. The service manager, service writer, or technician should take the time to explain exactly what needs to be done and why, using pictures and diagrams if necessary. You should get a clear, written estimate. If, during the job, it's found that additional work is necessary, you should be notified before the extra service is done.

On the tech's side, communication is again crucial. If your car has a problem, explain exactly when you notice it, what it sounds like, and so forth. Don't expect the technician to read your mind.

With today's unbelievably complicated cars, especially in the areas of emission controls and electronic systems, automotive technicians have to know far more than the practitioners of almost any other trade. And they have to learn about whole new systems every year. Respect them accordingly.

Profit on parts

It's a basic tenet of the automotive service business that making a profit on parts is absolutely necessary for financial survival. The markup is typically 40 to 50 percent. This shouldn't be a surprise. We know of no type of business where this practice is not followed.

By the way, it makes no

EXTRA: Certified Techs

Look for the ASE symbol, which stands for an organization known as the National Institute for Automotive Service Excellence. It gives technicians nationwide voluntary tests, and awards certificates, arm patches, and signs to those who pass. While this doesn't necessarily mean the tech will do a good job on your car, it is at least evidence that he or she knows the technical fine points and accepted procedures, and also cares enough to take the time to study and enhance his or her knowledge and professionalism.

sense to bring the parts necessary for the repair into the shop where you're having the work done—even though you might have come by them cheaply. As the old saying goes, it's like bringing bacon and eggs into the diner and asking the proprietor to cook them for you. The whole idea will be offensive to the shop owner, and, if there's a problem with the repair, you'll be reminded that it was done with your parts. Ergo, there'll probably be no warranty.

Miscellaneous

Random, but Important

88. What to carry with you

No, the average motorist shouldn't be lugging a ponderous mechanic's toolbox with him or her. You're not going to do a valve job on the side of the road, are you? But there are a few things that can save you time, frustration, and money if you happen to have them handy.

As we've mentioned in other sections, a can of aerosol tire inflator may keep you from getting dirty and overstressed. If you're willing to actually change a tire, you should have a 1-foot-square piece of 3/4-inch plywood with you, to place the jack on. You might also want to carry an X-type lug wrench,

which will give you more leverage on the wheel lug nuts, or perhaps a short length of pipe to increase the leverage available with the stock wrench. Just make sure any heavy hardware is stowed in such a way that it won't become a missile to hit you in the back of the head if you should run into something.

You will welcome a pair of work gloves from the dollar store if you have occasion to change a tire, or to do other dirty jobs.

A small container of pump or aerosol multipurpose lubricant can eliminate many problems from squeaks to difficult latches.

Carrying a quart or two of

>> **Carrying these few items, properly stowed, will save both money and frustration.**

the recommended oil wouldn't hurt, and it gives you the opportunity to buy it on sale at a discount store rather than at an inflated price at a convenience store on the highway. Stow that intelligently, too.

Typically, spare fuses come attached to the lid of the fuse box. If not, you could buy an assortment of the type your car uses (bayonet type on all late models) and keep it in your glove compartment.

If there's some component that tends to fail on your particular vehicle (in the old days, that might have been an ignition ballast resistor of Chrysler products, or, later, the TFI module of Ford ignition systems), get one when you have the opportunity and carry it with you.

A piece of tarpaulin or old carpet will give you a clean surface to lie on if you have to look underneath to check out the exhaust system, brakes, leaks, and the like.

You need a good flashlight, regardless.

All known authorities will tell you to stuff the car with flares or reflector triangles, a first-aid kit, and a fire extinguisher.

89. Battery parasitic drain

Even while parked, modern vehicles draw considerable amperage to keep their various computer memories alive. If you're going to store your car for a matter of months, disconnect the battery's negative cable (the battery will have a minus sign or "NEG" stamped on it where this cable connects) to avoid losing the charge. Typically, this will require

>> Storing your vehicle for a month or more? Be sure to disconnect the battery by removing the negative cable.

EXTRA: A Full Charge Amounts to Antifreeze

In subfreezing weather, a charged battery will keep fine, but the depleted electrolyte of a discharged one will freeze. This will ruin the internal plates and you'll have to buy a new battery.

the use of a 5/16-inch, 1/2-inch, or 10 mm wrench. Why the negative? Because if you should inadvertently touch a grounded component with the wrench in the process, you won't get an electrical arc strong enough to weld the tool to the car and burn you.

90. Gasoline goes stale

>> **Add a fuel stabilizer to the tank before you store your car to avoid serious starting and driveability problems.**

I f you're going to be storing your car for a matter of months, it would be a good idea to add a fuel stabilizer (the biggest brand is Stabil™) to the tank beforehand. Otherwise, the gasoline can form varnish and gum that may clog passages and cause other trouble in the fuel injection system, or, on older cars, inside the carburetor. Use the amount recommended on the bottle, and drive around a little to make sure it circulates throughout the system.

91. Interior mildew

Whether you call it mold, mildew, or fungus, this vegetable organism causes a bad smell and discoloration of anything it grows on. Like any plant, it needs moisture to grow, so the first order of business is to make sure the interior stays dry. If there's a leak, say, around the windshield, you'll be fighting a losing battle. The same is true if the tube that carries condensate from the air conditioner evaporator is clogged. All that water has nowhere to go but onto the carpet.

If you're storing your car for anything over a couple of weeks, better think about the best place to park it. You don't want to leave it in a low spot in the shade, or you'll be promoting mildew formation. We've seen people leave a bag of charcoal briquettes or an open box of baking soda in the car on the assumption that it will absorb water and odors—but we've never heard of this being scientifically tested. Couldn't hurt to try it, though.

Household bleach is the most potent weapon against whatever's growing in carpeting or upholstery, but you can easily take out the dye with the odor. If the material is a light color, experiment with a highly diluted solution on an area that's hidden from view and see if you get whitening or spots. If not, sponge the solution into the suspect area, then use a wet/dry shop vacuum to extract it.

92. Buying gasoline

Some people just like to fill 'er up with the premium whether or not it makes sense for his or her particular car. In most cases, however, that's simply a waste of money. There are only two situations where it's called for: One, if your owner's manual says so (you have taken the time to read at least its most important points, haven't you?), or two, if you're hearing detonation or "pinging." This sounds like ball bearings being poured into a hubcap, especially under high loads such as steep grades, or hard acceleration.

What you're buying when you opt for premium grades is a higher octane number (it's posted on the pump), which simply means the gasoline's additives cause it to burn more slowly and smoothly than regular. Your pistons get a push

>> **Gasoline's octane rating refers to its resistance to detonate (violently explode) in the cylinders.**

instead of the sharp blow that may occur under high loads with lower octane regular. Most late models incorporate what's known as a "knock sensor," which detects pinging/spark knock, and retards the timing of the ignition until the condition goes away. That will take the edge off the sparkling performance your car may be capable of, but this might not even be discernable unless you're timing yourself 0 to 60 with a stopwatch.

EXTRA: Buy Brand Name?

While oil companies naturally try to differentiate their brand of gasoline with advertising about how much better it'll make your car run, the truth is that there's not really much difference. All gasolines sold today contain an additive package that helps keep the fuel system, valves, and combustion chamber clean. Your choice will be mostly a matter of price and convenience.

93. When the battery must be disconnected . . .

If your car's battery terminals need to be cleaned and retightened, or the battery itself has died and must be replaced, you'll lose your preset radio stations and any other settings, such as those for the seat, steering wheel, and mirror positions, and, perhaps, the Powertrain control module (PCM)'s adaptive adjustments that make it run so well. That is, unless you connect an alternative voltage source to the electrical system.

For years, little devices that use a 9-volt battery and plug into the cigarette lighter have been available to hold settings. There are some problems with that today, however. In the first place, 9 volts isn't necessarily high enough to do the job.

Then, there's the amount of current that modern systems require–that little dry cell might run down before you get a chance to reconnect the vehicle battery.

So, you should use a big 12-volt source to do the job. If you have a spare car battery or one of those rechargeable jump-starting packs around,

connect its leads to the cable clamps (or, rings, as in the GM side-terminal style), positive to positive, and negative to negative. Since it can be difficult to work with the cables and keep the alligator clips connected, you might want to get an adapter that goes into the cigarette lighter and connect the leads to that.

94. Warranties

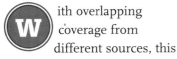ith overlapping coverage from different sources, this is a confusing subject. Every car comes with a warranty booklet, which you should take the time to read—it's stuffed in your glove compartment somewhere. The following will give you the most important basics and some handy tips.

New car
The warranty you got when you bought your new car probably runs for 3/36 (three years or 36,000 miles, whichever comes first) up to 5/60 depending on the automaker, and is usually referred to as "bumper-to-bumper" even though damage to body parts such as bumpers isn't covered.

During the first year, known as the "initial ownership period," just about anything

>> **Warranties are always complex, so take the time to read the information that came with your car.**

short of collision damage and egregious abuse will be fixed free by the new-car dealership, which will be reimbursed by the manufacturer. Thereafter, most big, expensive repairs will be covered, but the service department may refuse to do anything at no charge that's not explicitly spelled out in the warranty. In practice, however, the dealership will want to protect its reputation and future sales, so will often take care of nuisance items gratis.

Meanwhile, in most cases you're responsible for keeping up with maintenance according to the chart or schedule in your owner's manual. In other words, you pay for oil and filter changes (although some car makers now offer these free for a certain period after purchase), tire rotation, and anything else that's recommended. It's important to note that these jobs can be done at any service facility, or by you yourself if you're so inclined, not just at the dealership. Just be sure to save all the receipts for the work and the parts and fluids involved.

The replacement of normal wear items, such as brake linings, wiper blades, bulbs, key-fob batteries, etc., is up to you, but if something gives out in what you consider an unreasonably short time, talk to the dealer. There may be what's known as a "campaign" from the automaker on that item, which may not be publicized.

EXTRA: Fly by Night

If the extended warranty is offered by some company you've never heard of, don't even consider it. We've never seen an instance where one of these outfits paid without a fight, or even paid at all. Sometimes, when you need to contact the company you find that it's gone with the wind.

Or, the dealer may take care of it as goodwill.

Batteries and tires carry their own warranties. Replacement may be free for a year or two, but thereafter you get a prorated price discount based on what should have been the normal lifespan. Sometimes that doesn't work out to be a bargain compared to the good deals you can often find on these items in the vast automotive aftermarket, however.

When you bought your new car, chances are the dealer tried to sell you an extended powertrain warranty. If it's offered by the automaker itself, at least it's backed up by a reputable company. On the other hand, since this mostly covers internal engine and transmission parts, which will usually last far longer than any warranty given reasonable maintenance, there's really not much risk to the manufacturer. Yet the coverage costs a rather large amount. The cost/benefit ratio isn't particularly attractive.

Federal Emissions Warranty
In an effort to assure that today's clean-running cars stay that way, the Environmental Protection Agency (EPA) mandated that the automakers provide a warranty on systems that can affect the volume of

>> **The pollution-fighting catalytic converter in your exhaust system is covered under the Federal emissions warranty.**

pollutants a car spews into our precious atmosphere. It seems that very few people are even aware of this, and, if the truth be told, it isn't invoked all that often. The thing to remember about this warranty is that it only kicks in if your car has failed an EPA-approved state or local emissions test.

Basically, anything that has to do with how the engine runs is covered by the Federal Emission Warranty for 2/24 (3/50 in California), but your bumper-to-bumper would probably take care of most of that anyway. Exceptions are the catalytic converter in your exhaust system, and the Powertrain Control Module (PCM)—the engine management computer, which are both warranted for 8/80 (7/70 in California).

Special provisions for Partial Zero Emissions Vehicle (PZEV) hybrid electric vehicles are being developed at the time of this writing, so check current information.

95. Fail an emissions test?

I t's always a shock when you see the word "Fail," perhaps in big letters and circled. As if there weren't enough complications in modern life, now you're given a deadline for rectifying the situation, after which you become an outlaw. You're left scratching your head. Wasn't your car designed to meet the standards? Haven't you done your best to maintain it with regular oil changes and tune-ups? What's gone wrong? And, most important, what can you do to make it pass? Although the physics involved are very subtle and dynamic, fixing the problem is often quite straightforward.

Take a minute to read the rejection slip carefully. It will give you the test results for your car contrasted against acceptable limits. Note which of the "terrible trio"—hydrocarbons (HC), carbon monoxide (CO), or oxides of nitrogen (NOx)—is out of bounds. This should form the basis of your investigation.

Hydrocarbon emissions are simply unburned fuel (and maybe a little motor oil) being pumped raw into the exhaust system. Misfiring is the most likely culprit, and that can come from an ignition problem, or an internal engine failure that reduces compression. Another possibility is a mixture that's too lean to catch fire dependably either because of a fuel system malfunction or a vacuum leak. If a big HC number isn't from a miss, it's probably due to a rich mix.

So, worn or fouled spark

plugs are the first things to suspect. If you can feel a dead miss at idle, use special insulated pliers (grasp the rubber boot, not the wire itself) to pull plug wires one at a time to see if one in particular doesn't have any effect on smoothness. Don't do this on '96-and-up cars with OBD II as it will set a misfire code and turn on the Malfunction Indicator Lamp (MIL) on the dash. Remove and inspect that spark plug. If it's okay, use an ohmmeter to find out if the plug wire is "open" (has no continuity), then look the distributor cap over for heavy corrosion in the sockets, cracks, etc.

With the plug out, do a compression test—anything much less than 100 psi should be suspect (a valve may be burned). Also, look at the intake manifold to see if there's a vacuum tap in the runner to the problem cylinder. A leak here can lean out the air/fuel mixture (in other words, too little gasoline to too much air) to the point of misfire at idle.

CO is produced by incomplete combustion—the air/fuel charge is being ignited, but isn't burning properly or entirely. To put it another way, it's the result of combustion with an excess of fuel present. This is due, in most cases, to fuel system troubles that make the engine run rich, but intake air restrictions could affect it, too. It's important to note that some combustion is required or CO simply can't be created. You won't see a high CO reading if there's no spark.

In the days of carburetors, richness might have been due to any of these: an idle mixture screw that's open too much, a heavy float (the foam type may absorb gasoline, and the brass pontoon type can develop holes and fill up with fuel), a choke that stays on after the engine has warmed up, or a power valve that sticks in the open position. With the Electronic Fuel Injection (EFI) of today, perhaps the fuel pressure in the rail is too high due to a faulty fuel pressure regulator, or a cracked vacuum hose to the regulator.

Just about any car built since the early 1980s will have an electronic engine management system that controls the air/fuel mixture (among other things), so the sensors that feed information to the computer should be suspect. This, however, graduates into professional-level troubleshooting.

There are a couple of other things that can supply enough extra gasoline to put HC above the limit. One is the evaporative emissions control system that traps gasoline vapors (that would otherwise escape in the atmosphere), then meters it into the intake to be burned during off-idle modes. If it flows at idle, the mix will be too rich.

A final potential culprit in failing an emissions test is engine oil that's diluted with gasoline so that vapors are drawn through the Positive Crankcase Ventilation (PCV) system into the intake manifold. Smelling gas on the oil dipstick may tip you off to this, and an oil change will correct it temporarily. But you'll still have to find out why so much extra fuel is finding its way past the rings.

On a pre-computer-carbureted car, one way to get under the HC and CO limits is to retard the ignition timing, which slows the idle down and also provides a longer, hotter burn. Then, bring the idle speed back up to specs with the throttle-stop screw or idle stop solenoid, which will admit more air. Performance will be off, but you'll probably pass the test.

NOx has been a tough one. It forms when nitrogen (78 percent of the air we all breathe) combines with oxygen (21 percent of the atmosphere), which can happen *only* at very high combustion temperatures. The trouble is, many of the things that were initially done to cut HC and CO involved dramatically increasing the heat inside those cylinders, which created plenty of NOx. Fortunately, it was found that only the peak temperatures (over 2,500°F) produced this smog-promoting gas, not the long, hot burn that oxidized the other two pollutants. Introducing Exhaust Gas Recirculation (EGR) knocked the top off the temperature curve, thus putting NOx within bounds. One of the main reasons electronic engine management systems were developed (in the late 1970s) was to allow a three-way catalyst, which adds rhodium to the two-way catalyst's platinum and palladium, to further diminish this noxious emission.

The first things to suspect are an inoperative EGR valve, if your car has one (perhaps the vacuum line is cracked, or the internal diaphragm has ruptured) and carbon-clogged EGR passages. Try applying vacuum to the valve, or simply move its pin, at idle. If the engine starts to run roughly or stalls, the valve is okay and the passages are at least partially open. Remove the valve and dig out all the deposits you can.

There's a good chance that the catalytic converter is no longer capable of reducing NOx, but determining that requires high-tech diagnosis best left to a professional. There's another possibility that you can deal with, however: heavy carbon deposits in the combustion chambers and on the backs of the intake valves.

Believe it or not, these deposits can raise the compression ratio enough to cause the hot flash that forms NOx, and will also interfere with the carefully engineered swirl pattern that makes the incoming mixture burn evenly.

Numerous treatments have been devised to avoid the huge job of removing the cylinder head and manually cleaning the combustion chambers, piston tops, and the valves (even blasting with walnut shell fragments!), but the only one suitable for the do-it-yourselfer is chemical treatment. The most basic approach is to pour an additive into the gas tank. Given a high enough concentration and sufficient time, this actually helps. A more thorough job, however, can be achieved with the injection of detergent- or solvent-based cleaners directly into the intake stream.

In older cars without a knock sensor, ignition timing that's too far advanced so that detonation is occurring can cause NOx levels to rise. A switch to premium may help.

EXTRA: Pick Your Day

Moisture-laden air can lower NOx output by as much as 30 percent, so you might consider visiting the test site on a rainy day. You should still correct the root cause, however.

Exhaust System

This relatively crude plumbing channels the burned gases the engine creates back to the tailpipe where it is released into the atmosphere. It consists of an exhaust manifold (two on V6s and V8s, one for each bank of cylinders), a head pipe or "Y" pipe from there to the muffler (some cars have a second small muffler called a resonator that quiets things down a little more), then the tailpipe. This assembly is suspended along the way by various hangers, usually with rubber elements that help isolate the vibrations that cause noise. Also, you'll find a catalytic converter somewhere between the manifold and the muffler. Made of stainless steel, it has catalytic agents inside that reduce a vehicle's emissions.

96. Rattles

There's not much clearance between the components and the frame rails, suspension parts, and so on, with the way the components are tucked up into the chassis as they snake toward the rear. So, there is potential for the unintended contact that causes rattles as the hangers stretch or break over time. There are also various heat shields of light aluminum that can come loose and clatter. It's easy to replace a hanger, but not so easy to reaffix a heat shield.

Another type of rattle occurs when the baffles inside the muffler break loose. Replacement is the only cure.

97. Leaks

If the escaping gases seep into the passenger cabin, an exhaust leak can be dangerous. Even if not, it's noisy. The sound can range from a little ticking to an ear-shattering roar.

Since the exhaust system is subject to cycles of heating and cooling, vibration, corrosion, and physical damage from scraping the road, its integrity is always at risk. A large leak, such as from an open connection, a broken pipe, or a rusted-through muffler will be easily visible. Careful examination will be needed to locate smaller leaks, such as at a connection, or through pinholes in pipes or the muffler, a crack in the exhaust manifold, or a break in the gasket between the manifold and the cylinder head. If you pass your hand over likely areas, you'll feel the escaping gases, but be extremely careful not to actually touch that hot metal.

Sometimes a connection can be tightened, or new clamps can be added to choke off a leak, but generally a part will need to be replaced.

98. Temporary fix

If one of the exhaust-system hangers snaps, a pipe breaks, or a connection comes loose so that the muffler or a pipe is dragging on the road, stop ASAP and use whatever's handy to hold the system up until you can get to a shop. Otherwise, you're apt to lose the whole thing when it might only need a simple repair. Any kind of metal wire or strap, or even a steel coat hanger, will do. Just try to keep it from falling off until you can get service.

Where to Get Info

99. If you've lost your owner's manual

You've noticed that throughout this book we've admonished you to look things up in your owner's manual. Given human nature and the vagaries of modern life, though, there's a good chance that you've lost yours somewhere along the way.

Replacements are available. The most widely accepted place to try is www.helminc.com (Helm Incorporated, 14310 Hamilton Avenue, Highland Park, MI 48203), or call the company at 800-782-4356 (Fax: 313-865-5927). If your car isn't on the list, you can visit the parts department of the dealership that sells your make and order one.

100. Factory service manuals

These are comprehensive, but expensive and bulky. Easily available, though. Again, you can go through Helm Incorporated (see #99, pg 168), or the car dealer.

Regardless of how you come by it, a factory service manual for your year, make, and model will contain subtleties that no other source of information can match.

EXTRA: Alternative Sources

If you're computer and Internet capable, you might be able to find exactly what you want through a site search, perhaps on eBay, or from several automotive literature companies. This may save you a considerable amount of money.

101. Aftermarket tech info

If you're an automotive do-it-yourselfer, you've probably at least heard of Chilton, Clymer, Haynes, and the famous MOTOR manuals. They may cover a specific make and model for a span of years, or all domestics, or imports, also for some particular length of time. These are boiled down from the factory service literature. The editors choose which subjects they believe will be of use to you, then, if they're doing their job properly, streamline the tedious industrial-style writing so that it's more readable and compact.

These can be helpful, but we've always felt shortchanged. Many points that we consider extremely important have often been missing, or misinterpreted. Typically, the editors are just

that, editors, not automotive service technicians, so they may not recognize the gaps. If you're not going to get in too deeply, though, this kind of reference may help guide your maintenance and repair efforts.

Much of the above may also be available on CD, or even DVD, from aftermarket publishers. It'll probably be identical content, but a search feature will make things easier to find.

If we may be immodest enough to say so, another great source of car care information can be found at www.popularmechanics.com. While the fully illustrated articles on the site won't apply specifically to your car, you will find the generic information extremely helpful, complete, and timely. Under "Automotive," just click "Car Care Channel," then "Saturday Mechanic Monthly Car Repair Features," and you'll get a huge list of titles, which should cover most of your automotive questions.

Beyond that, there's Alldata (www.alldata.com), which makes manufacturers' service information available by means of paid access to its web site. This even includes Technical Service Bulletins (TSBs), which are issued from time to time by carmakers to address certain repair issues, and can solve mysterious problems. Access starts at $25 for the first vehicle, then an additional $15 each for others.

Car Care Log

DATA ON YOUR VEHICLE

Year/Make/Model

Engine size

Tire size

Recommended tire inflation pressure

Engine oil capacity
   With filter
   Without filter

Oil filter type/number

Air filter type/number

Cooling system capacity

Recommended antifreeze type

Maintenance and repair records

To my wife, Carol, who put up with my shirking family duties, and my daughter, Kira, who hoped I wouldn't make this boring.

Thanks to Paul Weissler, well-known automotive technical writer, who didn't want me to miss anything important, to Mark Boege, super technician and owner of American Automotive, for his sound advice and generosity in the use of his shop, and to Lieutenant William H. Leeper of the Florida Highway Patrol, Troop G Jacksonville, for his helpful comments.

Index

Accidents, 97–100
  fires from, 97–98
  landing in water,
    99–100
  not moving from, 97
  what to say, 99
  who to call, 98–99
Aftermarket tech info,
  170–171
Air conditioning odors,
  87–88
Air filter/ducts, 16, 31–32
Alignment. See
  Steering/suspension
Alternator, 21

Battery, 22
  charging, 40–41
  draining/storing,
    152–153
  installing new, 41–42
  terminals/cables, 22,
    27–28
  warning light, 57–58
  when to disconnect,
    156–157
Belts, 18, 29–30, 131
Bouncing/leaning car,
  70–71
Brakes
  changing fluid,
    136–138
  checking/adding fluid,
    26
  fluid leaks, 56–57
  master cylinder, 15, 26

pad wear indicators,
  76–77
power brake booster,
  15
pulling car to one
  side, 68, 69
pulsating, 71–72
warning lamps, 61–62
Breakdowns. See also
  Warning lamps
  brake fluid leaks,
    56–57
  cooling system leaks,
    51–52
  flat tires, 45–51
  installing new battery,
    41–42
  jump-starting, 39–40
  no-crank/no-fire
    starting failures,
    36–39
  no power to wheels,
    43–44
  oil leaks, 52–53
  power steering fluid
    leaks, 55–56
  safety precautions,
    34–35, 46–49
  sudden stop, 43
  transmission fluid
    leaks, 54
  who to call, 35–36

Camshaft cover, 19
Carburetor, 16
Car care log, 172

Catalytic converter, 19,
  160, 164–165
Check engine light,
  59–61
Cleaning car
  interior, 85–87, 112
  washing/waxing,
    138–141
Clutch, 23
Coil, ignition, 19
Cooling system
  changing coolant,
    127–128
  checking/adding
    coolant, 25
  hoses, 30
  leaks, 51–52
  overflow reservoir, 15
  radiator, 19, 31
Cylinder head cover, 19

Dashboard lights. See
  Warning lamps
Distributor, 19
Distributorless-ignition,
  19
DLC (Data Link
  Connector), 61
Door-latch strikers, 104
Drain holes, 86–87, 144
Driveshaft problems,
  69–70
Driving tips
  accelerating easily, 96
  defensive driving,
    92–93

reducing speed, 96–97
slippery conditions,
93–94
DTC (Diagnostic Trouble
Code), 61
Durability, 122–124

EGR (Exhaust Gas
Recirculation), 164
Electrical system. *See also*
Battery
components, 19,
21–23
jump-starting, 39–40
no-crank/no-fire
starting failures,
36–39
Emergencies. *See*
Accidents; Breakdowns
Emissions test, failing,
161–165
Exhaust system
leaks, 167
manifold, 19
rattles, 166
temporary fixes, 168

Factory service manuals,
169
Fires, 97–98
Firewall, 22
Fluids, 24–26
Fuel
buying/octane levels,
155–156
mileage, 95–96
stabilizer for, 153–154
Fuel injection, 16,
162–163
Fuel pump, 16
Fuses, 23

Gas cap, loose, 60
Gasoline. *See* Fuel
Gear lube, 132

Headlights, 117–121
Hoods/hood supports,
12–13, 105
Hoses, 30

Idle, rough, 73
Ignition system, 19–20,
73, 74–76, 101, 130

Jacking procedures, 46–49
Jump-starting, 39–40

Keys
fobs/remotes, 103
not turning in
ignition, 101
spare, hiding, 102

Lights, 117–121
Limp-in mode, 74
Locks, power, 108

MAF (Mass Air Flow)
sensor, 32
Maintenance. *See specific
topic*
Manuals, 168–171
Mechanical tour, 14–23
Mechanics, dealing with,
144–147
Mildew (mold, fungus),
85–87, 154
Mileage, calculating,
95–96
MIL (Malfunction
Indicator Lamp), 59–61,
73, 74

Mirror, reattaching,
114–115
Muffler, 19

Noises
clunks/thumps, 77–80
rattles/buzzes, 81–85,
166
tapping/knocking,
80–81

OBD (On-Board
Diagnostics) system,
59–61, 73
Odors, 85–88, 154
Oil
carrying extra, 150–151
changing, 124–127
checking/adding,
24–25
dipstick, 14
filter, 17
leaks, 52–53
pressure, warning
light, 58
Owner's manual
replacements, 168
Oxygen sensors, 74, 75

Paint chips, 141–142
PCM (Powertrain Control
Module), 32, 59, 160
PCV (Positive Crankcase
Ventilation) valve, 20,
163
Power locks, 108
Power steering
fluid/leaks, 16, 55–56
Power windows, 106–107
Professionals, dealing
with, 144–147

Rack-and-pinion steering, 23
Radiator. *See* Cooling system
Rattles/buzzes, 81–85, 166
Recirculating ball steering, 23
Reference manuals, 168–171
Relays, 23
Repair shops, dealing with, 144–147
Rust spots, 142–143

Safety precautions, 34–35, 46–49. *See also* Accidents
Serpentine belts, 18, 29–30
Service manuals, 168–172
Shocks/struts, 70–71
Skidding, 93–94
Slippery conditions, 93–94
Sluggish performance, 74–76
Smells, 85–88, 154
Smoke smells/filters, 89
Solenoid, 21
Spark plugs, 19, 75, 130, 162–163
Starter, 21
Steering/suspension
   alignment, 64–66, 68–69
   gear, 23
   noises, 77–80
   pulling to one side, 67–69
   shocks/struts, 70–71
   wandering during, 64–66
   wheel, crooked, 65
Stops, sudden, 43
Supplies, to carry, 150–152

Technicians, dealing with, 144–147
Throttle body, 16
Timing-belt replacement, 131
Tires. *See also* Steering/suspension
   balancing, 69
   buying, 134–135
   chains for, 94
   flat, changing/fixing, 45–51
   inflating, 50, 67, 133
   rotating, 133
Transmission
   breakdown/repair, 43–44
   changing fluid, 131–132
   checking/adding fluid, 25
   fluid leaks, 54
   oil dipstick, 14
Tune-ups, 129

Vacuum lines, 20
Valve cover, 19
Vibrations, 69–70
Voltage regulator, 21

Warning lamps
   ABS/brake system, 61–62
   charging system, 57–58
   check engine, 59–61
   oil pressure, 58
Warranties, 157–160
Washing/waxing car, 138–141
Windows, power, 106–107
Windshield
   bull's-eyes, 113–114
   haze inside, 112
   washer fluid reservoir, 15
   washers, 111–112
   wiper motor, 22
   wipers, 109–111